HOW TO DEFEND books AND WHY

I0109915

DANNY CAINE

Microcosm Publishing
Portland, Ore | Cleveland, Ohio

HOW TO DEFEND books AND WHY

Book Bans and How We Fight Them

DANNY CAINE

Microcosm Publishing
Portland, Ore | Cleveland, Ohio

How to Defend Books and Why: Book Bans and How We Fight Them
© Danny Caine, 2026
This edition © Microcosm Publishing, 2026
First edition, 5,000 copies, first published June 2, 2026
Edited by Lex Orgera
Cover by Ron Kretsch
Book design by Sarah Koch with Joe Biel
ISBN 9781648414084
This is Microcosm #963

For a catalog, write or visit:
Microcosm Publishing
2752 N Williams Ave.
Portland, OR 97227
(503)799-2698

All the news from the misfits in print at Microcosm.Pub/Newsletter
Get more copies of this book at Microcosm.Pub/HowtoDefendBooks
Get more books by this author at Microcosm.Pub/DannyCaine

EU Safety Information: microcosmpublishing.com/gpsr

To join the ranks of high-class stores that feature Microcosm titles, talk to your rep:
In the U.S. COMO (Atlantic), ABRAHAM (Midwest), sales@microcosm.pub (Texas,
Oklahoma, Louisiana, Arkansas), IMPRINT (Pacific), TURNAROUND (UK, Africa,
Europe, Middle East), UTP/MANDA (Canada), NEWSOUTH (Australia/New
Zealand), APD (Asia), HarperCollins (India), and FAIRE in the gift trade.

Did you know that you can buy our books directly from us at sliding scale rates?
Support a small, independent publisher and pay less than Amazon's price at Micro-
cosm.Pub.

Global labor conditions are bad, and our roots in industrial Cleveland in the '70s and
'80s made us appreciate the need to treat workers right. Therefore, our books are
MADE IN THE USA.

Microcosm's workers and authors are paid solely from book sales. If you downloaded this book from some sketchy part of the Internet or picked up what appears to be a bootleg, please support our hardworking team by purchasing a copy directly from us and encouraging your communities to do the same. Paying for our books and zines helps us publish work that's far better than anything AI can come up with. Additionally, a 2025 MIT study revealed that AI inhibits humanity's critical thinking ability. Since critical thinking is one of our core values, we prohibit any use of our books to "train" generative artificial "intelligence" (AI) technologies, because seriously, WTF?

MICROCOSM·PUBLISHING

ABOUT THE PUBLISHER

MICROCOSM PUBLISHING is Portland's most diversified publishing house and distributor, with a focus on the colorful, authentic, and empowering. Our books and zines have put your power in your hands since 1996, equipping readers to make positive changes in their lives and in the world around them. Microcosm emphasizes skill-building, showing hidden histories, and fostering creativity through challenging conventional publishing wisdom with books and bookettes about DIY skills, food, bicycling, gender, self-care, and social justice. What was once a distro and record label started by Joe Biel in a drafty bedroom was determined to be *Publishers Weekly*'s fastest-growing publisher of 2022 and #3 in 2023, and is now among the oldest independent publishing houses in Portland, OR, and Cleveland, OH. We are a politically moderate, centrist publisher in a world that has inched to the right for the past 80 years.

Global labor conditions are bad, and our roots in industrial Cleveland in the '70s and '80s made us appreciate the need to treat workers right. Therefore, our books are MADE IN THE USA.

CONTENTS

Dedicated to the librarians of the United States, and in memory of those in Palestine who have been killed or otherwise silenced.

INTRODUCTION: BOOKS UNDER SIEGE

THE ACTUAL HOAX

On January 24, 2025, Donald Trump's Department of Education (DOE) declared that it was ending "Biden's Book Ban Hoax."[1] The defiant press release also announced that the DOE was dismissing 11 complaints about what it calls "so-called book bans." The cases in question aren't about banning books, according to the press release, but rather "a school district's removal of age-inappropriate books from its libraries." In describing its hasty review and dismissal of the cases (the press release came five days after Trump's inauguration), the press release declares, "Attorneys quickly confirmed that books are not being 'banned,' but [rather] school districts, in consultation with parents and community stakeholders, have established commonsense processes by which to evaluate and remove age-inappropriate materials." Here's what those "commonsense processes" look like: In the 2021-2022 school year, PEN America reported 2,532 attempts to restrict access to certain books, most of which had been professionally reviewed for age appropriateness.[2] In the next school year, that number ballooned to 3,362. Then, for the 2023-2024 school year, that number nearly tripled to 10,046, an easy all-time record for the number of attempts at banning books. But numbers, drastic as they are, are only one way to look at the crisis (which is a real crisis, despite what Trump's DOE says).

In actual practice, here are a few ways these "commonsense processes" manifest: Hostile takeovers of school boards. Defunding public libraries. Turning school libraries into discipline centers. Grown adults humiliating and shouting at brave teenagers who are trying to give public comment at library board meetings. Individual parents bulk challenging hundreds of books at a time. Adults reading out-of-context passages into city council microphones to try to spook local politicians into banning books. People building websites with the explicit purpose of making this hostile and deliberately ignorant misreading possible. Mislabeling anything that even addresses sex as "pornography," and the librarians who foster access to it as "groomers." The Republican establishment funneling huge amounts of money into the so-called "grassroots" groups driving this effort, even while the groups claim that their money comes from T-shirt sales. Librarians being harassed, doxxed, made to fear for their safety. Underlying all this are two factors: first, a growing desire on the Right to eliminate public education altogether, replacing it with private Christian schools that nonetheless receive government funding. Second, nearly every book targeted by this well-organized and well-funded movement is either by a queer author, by a BIPOC author, or intended for queer or BIPOC readers.

Book bans are not the hoax. Rather, the hoax is the right-wing narrative that all this is happening to enshrine so-called "parents' rights." Another hoax: that this is only about books. Indeed, what we'll call the book ban crisis is actually about the dismantling of secular education and the targeted elimination of identities that fall outside the Christian nationalist worldview. Any attempt to deny this? That's the actual hoax.

THE CHILLING EFFECT

The pressure began before I even had the job. Before I was the 10th grade English teacher in Room 9 at Smithville High School in Smithville, Ohio, I was a college sophomore education student doing a short field placement with Mrs. Fischer, my predecessor in Room 9. One day during that field placement she and I were having a meeting, strategizing for an upcoming unit I'd be teaching about King Arthur. I suggested the idea of screening *Monty Python and the Holy Grail* before discussing with students the ways that the Pythons deconstruct and tweak the Arthurian myths.

"You can't do that," snapped the irascible Mrs. Fischer.

"Why not?" I asked, taken aback.

"It would never fly here," she replied.

"The movie is rated PG-13, and these are 16-year-olds," I suggested.

"Can't do it," she replied, curt.

"Really? The movie is just goofy, it's not inappropriate," I pleaded. Mrs. Fischer's prickly manner often stoked my own argumentativeness, but Smithville was no place for such an attitude, especially from someone like me.

Mrs. Fischer told me, in a way that suggested there would be no further discussion, "This is just not a place where you can show a movie like that."

Eventually, I graduated and got my Ohio substitute certification. I subbed a few times at Smithville, which was a quick 10-minute drive down the road from the small liberal arts college I had just graduated from. My first time subbing, I was given no lesson plans by the head football coach, on the cusp of retirement. The star quarterback fell asleep on the floor during third period. Mrs. Fischer and I would maintain our thorny but mostly amicable chats on the days I subbed at Smithville, and one day in

February she told me she was retiring effective immediately and that I should apply to finish out the year as her long-term sub. That's exactly what happened, and I quickly got to work putting my stamp on the Smithville 10th grade English curriculum, and more specifically the classroom library Mrs. Fischer had left me.

Talking to the sophomores about what they wanted to read was quite enlightening—and often, the answer didn't line up with the dusty old paperbacks Mrs. Fischer had left me. It's been many years, so I don't remember a ton of the books, but the library I inherited definitely included a hardcover, vaguely Christmas-y illustrated version of Robert Frost's "Stopping by Woods on a Snowy Evening." A beat-up mass market of *The Once and Future King*. An abridged illustrated classics *Huckleberry Finn*. Lots of that kind of thing. Many of my students were happy with the eternally disintegrating *Harry Potter* series perpetually on loan to one student or another. Others, though, wanted more. They were interested in books like *Crank* by Ellen Hopkins and *Speak* by Laurie Halse Anderson—gritty books that were honest about teenage experiences, warts and all. Books that directly confronted the pain and sadness of being a teenager. I would haunt the area's used bookstores, searching for the stuff they wanted, stocking the classroom library out of my own pocket. Once a year, the Friends of the Library would fill a building at the fairground with dollar paperbacks, and I would always leave with boxes. One year I found most of John Green's novels and instantly added them to the library. They were constantly checked out. My library never came under scrutiny from the administrators. I wonder if I escaped scrutiny simply because the most controversial books were always checked out and never lingering on the shelves.

Even though my library escaped scrutiny, much else happened to create a chilling effect, or pressure to self-censor what I could say and do in my classroom and elsewhere. Vaguely defined (or even undefined) "community standards" were, again and again, used as a cudgel to control my behavior and my classroom discussions. My first year at Smithville, I taught a mythology class. As the December break approached, I decided to spend a class period teaching the students how to play dreidel, explaining the Hanukkah myth in the process. I should say here that I am Jewish, and as far as I know, I was the only Jew in Smithville High School at the time (and maybe even in Smithville proper). When I returned in January, I was summoned to the principal's office. There had been parent phone calls about the dreidel lesson. My boss wouldn't tell me who called or what they said. Just to be careful. Consider "community standards."

There were other ways that these community standards were imposed: For instance, since I'm incapable of coaching anything, it fell to me to oversee student council, which meant organizing each year's homecoming dance. One year, a tight budget meant I would have to DJ the homecoming dance myself on a rented PA. I was handed a list of verboten songs that should under no circumstance be played. At the top of the list was "I Kissed a Girl" by Katy Perry. Stapled to the list was an explanation of Smithville's "community standards" about dancing. Any student caught "freaking" or "grinding" was to be sent to the office to call home and explain that they'd been kicked out of the dance. The night of the dance, the office phone had a line out the door and down the hall. I knew for a fact that nearly all these students were heading to a risky, boozy barn party, but I was powerless to do anything from my perch playing nothing more edgy than The Electric Slide.

Speaking of homecoming, every single pep rally at Smithville opened with a prayer, led by the 12th-grade English teacher, concluding with "in Jesus's name we pray, amen." I spent many planning periods complaining about this in the classroom of my lone close friend in Smithville, a queer teacher living mostly in the closet. At some point my fury about the prayers boiled over so much that I printed the Supreme Court's decision in *Engel v. Vitale*—the decision that banned compulsory prayer in schools—and highlighted several relevant parts. I showed it to my boss. He heard me out, and then told me, "That's just not how this town works." As if community standards superseded actual legal precedent. That's the thing, though. A certain kind of right-wing religious person thinks they answer first to "community standards," usually a euphemism for "Christian doctrine," and only after that to the laws and precedents of the United States. They expect everyone else to follow along—and screw you if you don't.

I don't want to imply that communities can't impose their own standards and expectations and values. Of course they can. But if the process of imposing community standards ignores or silences vulnerable community members in favor of those in power, that's a kind of violence. And that's what was happening in Smithville. The town's baked-in homophobia and intolerance of those outside the norm was a daily reality for me and for countless students who didn't fit into the mold that Smithville's powerful decided were community standards. Even the guidance counselor, in theory a person who could provide solace to students who felt oppressed by the homophobic atmosphere, propagated the hatred. These were the years when *Glee* was still on TV, and many of the staff were fans. One beautiful spring day, I was doing some reading time outside with my class when the guidance counselor, Conrad, came up to me. He told me he liked last night's episode of *Glee*, but he was beginning to feel like "the gay agenda" was taking over the show. My ability to respond to this was hamstrung by the fact that I was in front of my students. It was a complicated and humiliating moment—humiliating mainly because my shock and the complicatedness of the situation's politics froze me enough that I didn't respond at all.

Out of this atmosphere, I let a few kids eat lunch in my room. They were misfits, the few goths or nerds that were at that school. They'd lounge around, munch on Goldfish, shoot the shit. I don't want to paint myself like a savior here—I was far from a perfect teacher, and more often than not it was deeply annoying to have teenagers in my room during some of the rare minutes reserved for my own quiet time—but I felt like it was one little thing I could do to carve out some space for students who were never asked what they thought "community standards" should be.

The last October I was at Smithville I decided to do a lesson about banned books for Banned Books Week. I wanted to shock the students with statistics about how often their beloved *Harry Potter* books had been challenged. I was feeling feisty when plotting this lesson, so I checked out a copy of *And Tango Makes Three* from the local public library, planning to lead a story time to show that the book was a sweet story about penguins, not dangerous in the least. But when that part of the lesson arrived, I looked down at the book on the desk. I paused for a moment, then decided not to read the book at all. Not to even talk about it. I had them write in their journals instead. My deeply-held convictions— that representation in books is important, that books shouldn't be banned, that teens should read about a range of experiences including those that feel relevant to them—faded away. It was just plain fear. I was afraid of my boss walking in, afraid of being disciplined, afraid of losing my job, afraid of what some students might say. Once again, I silenced myself instead of standing up for those outside the town's strict Christian mandate. The repressive and restrictive "community standards" that those in power worked so hard to maintain had created a chilling effect. The chilling effect led me to censor myself. This hurt me, and I'm sure it hurt the students in various ways. It hurt the students that fled to my room instead of the cafeteria every day. It also hurt the students who internalized it. It even hurt the student who, for a public speaking unit about prejudice, stood in front of the class and said, in all seriousness, "If gay people don't want to be bullied, they should just stop being gay."

That was 15 years ago. In many ways, there are countless Smithvilles today. Damaging as my time at Smithville was, it is absolutely nothing compared to what teachers deal with under the current assault of the Christian nationalist far right as they desperately try to impose their "community standards" on the entire nation, starting with school libraries. For one thing, very few people feel the need to keep their prejudices private anymore. In school board and city council meeting rooms across the country, people from the religious right are stepping to the mic to say the quiet part out loud. This has only intensified the assault on everyone who falls outside the religious right's idea of how to live correctly, and it starts with books.

The story of my brief and painful tenure at Smithville in many ways mirrors the high school experience of Philomena Polefrone, the brilliant and tenacious crusader tasked with fighting book bans on behalf of the American Booksellers Association. One day in 2024, as the assault on books was reaching heights I never thought I'd see, Polefrone tells me her "supervillain origin story." She was uncertain of her identity in high school. One place this pressure felt eased was in the classroom of a particular English teacher. Polefrone tells me that the teacher "was a really close ally to me and a ton of other students in the school—students who either knew they were queer or trans, or didn't know that they were queer or trans (in my case)." Like the students who ate lunch in my room, Polefrone had a teacher who provided a space for her to be herself when spaces like that were rare. That space fell apart, though, when the teacher was forced out of her job because of books she assigned. "It was a choose-your-own-assignment type of thing where you chose from a list of books," Polefrone tells me. One of the books on the list caught the attention of local parents, who decided it was pornographic. Polefrone strongly challenges this characterization of the book, and she's right—slapping an inaccurate label of "pornography" on a book that simply discusses sexuality or queer identity is a common tactic among book banners. Polefrone says that, rather than being obscene, the book "was just poetry that captured the full scope of the human experience, including sexuality." Still, it didn't matter. Even if it's desperately inaccurate, the accusation of providing pornography to children is difficult to shake. That's precisely why they use the word. "Community standards" don't allow that kind of thing, after all. So, the teacher was either fired or left her job— Polefrone doesn't remember, and it doesn't matter. The chilling effect led to the closure of a safe space. Polefrone says, "I was a queer kid who found a home in a classroom in a safe space that didn't exist after a teacher was thrown out."

Now, as the ABA's book ban specialist, Polefrone has her work cut out for her. While her story and mine are individual instances from years ago, this kind of thing is desperately common these days. Right-wing crusaders, acting under the misleading mantle of "parents' rights" (these rights are only reserved for certain parents: parents like them) have set about creating the same kind of chilling effect in thousands of school districts, libraries, and bookstores across the country. They label important books "pornography," they label teachers and librarians "groomers," and they file hundreds of frivolous book challenges. And here's the thing about the chilling effect—it doesn't even matter if the challenges are administratively successful. Under the chilling effect, a challenge is already a ban. Many libraries remove books as soon as they're challenged, for one thing. For another, if a teacher or librarian is harassed enough, they do their own silent book banning. I never did read *And Tango Makes Three* to my students. The chilling effect at Smithville was enough to make me my own book banner.

If this were just about removing access to books, it would be crisis enough. But, of course, it's about more than books. I left Smithville after three years, simply unable to operate under the chilling effect anymore. In many cases, I'm not sure what happened to the students who ate lunch in my classroom. It seems unlikely that the Smithville powers-that-be would hire another teacher who operated outside of their community standards or even viewed those standards with a healthy cynicism. Similarly, Polefrone mourns not only the loss of a teacher but the loss of the space that teacher provided. As our conversation reaches an emotional peak, Polefrone tells me, "It is no exaggeration to say that book bans will increase suicide rates among queer kids. Book bans are a way of saying, 'not only are you not welcome in this school, we don't think that you should be welcome to exist, that you are so heinous that you cannot be represented in literature in public.'"

The last day of 10th grade is never going to be a productive or structured day. It's a day for screening movies, for loose conversations. My last day of my last year at Smithville, I decided to disperse the classroom library. I told the students to take what they wanted. There was much joy as they browsed the shelves and filled their backpacks with books. In a possible preview of my eventual career as a bookseller, I handed some students specific books—you, Tyler, need to read *Catcher in the Rye*. Savannah, you need to read *The Perks of Being a Wallflower*. After I left, there would be little I could do to carve a safer space for them in a place like Smithville. But I could send them home with a book that they could call theirs forever. Some would call this act "grooming," a deeply offensive and incorrect accusation. I was simply trying to help them see themselves in books, in the perhaps idealistic hope that a bit of recognition could help point them towards a better future. Maybe even a future where they could fight back against the oppressive harm caused to them in the name of "community standards," "parents' rights," or any number of other dog whistles that really just mean Christian nationalism.

Maybe one of them could end up like Nick Higgins, who started as a part-time library worker, eventually becoming a vigilante distributing books in Rikers Island jails before ascending to head librarian at Brooklyn Public Library, in the process becoming a leader in the fight against book bans.

Maybe one of them could end up like Valerie Kohler and Charley Rejsek, standing up to fight the state of Texas in the name of the freedom to read, all the while waging a war for hearts and minds in their communities, one conversation at a time.

Maybe one of them could end up like Lawrence Ferlinghetti, publishing cutting-edge literature and fighting a successful war in the media and in his bookshop on behalf of the right of such literature to exist. Or maybe they could end up like Elaine Katzenberger or Paul Yamazaki, carrying Ferlinghetti's mantle to the next generation, in the process giving voice to people struggling to share their voices at all.

Maybe one of them could end up like Mosab Abu Toha or Atef Abu Saif, with the courage to create witness-bearing literature in the literal face of death, sharing stories of genocide from the midst of that genocide and fighting against the deadly forces trying to silence those stories.

Maybe one of them could end up like Lauren Groff, who could easily and happily continue writing prize-winning novels for the rest of her career but, instead, also opened a bookstore to serve as a beacon of freedom amid an anti-book, anti-intellectual, anti-freedom fascist takeover of Florida.

Maybe one of them could end up like Tara Lipsyncki, a Utah drag queen and community organizer who worked to bring communal joy and beauty to children's story times at her bookstore and community hub despite regular harassment and even death threats.

One student to emerge from such a restrictive environment for sure ended up becoming a crusader to make sure it never happens again—Philomena Polefrone, who not only valiantly fights book bans every day, but also has literally written the book about how to fight them.

This book tells the story of the current book ban crisis, the worst in more than a generation. It also tells the story of the people who are fighting back.

THE QUICKLY UNFOLDING CRISIS

Admittedly, this book was difficult to write because there was simply so much happening while I was writing it. Every day brought some sort of news story about a new book ban, piece of legislation, or other attempt to curtail access to books. Just as it seemed like right-to-read crusaders had curbed the damage from the 2023 Texas legislative session, the 2025 session ramped up with even more damaging bills introduced. While I was beginning my edits, the Supreme Court issued a decision in *Mahmoud v. Taylor* that allowed parents to opt their children out of school discussions of books with LGBTQ+ characters and themes. The activist organization Authors Against Book Bans called the decision in *Mahmoud v. Taylor* "a tragic failure for both the right to read and the rights of LGBTQIA+ people." Just to keep track of all this, let alone write a coherent book about it, felt impossible. When I asked Philomena about how she kept track of everything, she said that at times "My whole brain is just bill numbers, just rattling around in there and then trying to keep track of each bill's status and peculiarities." So, I suppose that's one of the first points I'd like to make: This is happening everywhere, and it's happening a lot. There are a lot of ways to curtail access to books, and the book banners are doing it all. Even if you think it's all happening in Texas and Florida, I assure you that somewhere close to you, someone is attacking your freedom to read. I cannot provide an up-to-the-minute comprehensive index of all these assaults, for the simple reason that I'm turning in the final draft of this book more than six months before you'll read it. Instead of a comprehensive tick-tock account, I'll opt to tell representative stories that try to capture overarching truths of the crisis. In addition to reading these stories, I invite you to find the current data about where you are, as well as efforts to locally fight back.

THE ORIGINS OF THE CRISIS

Here's a rough sketch of how things started, at least from the book-banning perspective. At the peak of the Covid-19 pandemic in 2020 and 2021, the far right in America coalesced around resistance to mask mandates and other public health initiatives. You may remember death threats to Dr. Anthony Fauci or the plot to kidnap Michigan governor Gretchen Whitmer. As mask mandates faded away and the pandemic receded slightly, a few things happened. First, these far-right folks were emboldened to make their rhetoric and actions more violent and extreme in the wake of the January 6, 2021, attack on the U.S. Capitol. Second, education moved into the home as schooling went remote to mitigate the pandemic. Where, once, whatever happened in classrooms stayed in the classroom, now learning happened at the dining room table in full earshot of parents. Some parents didn't like what they heard, specifically regarding gender identity, diversity, and lessons about things like slavery and the Holocaust. Nick Higgins, head librarian at the Brooklyn Public Library, summarizes it well when he talks about the radicalization around the pandemic-era kitchen table:

> It was almost like a perfect storm, a potential radicalization of people who were looking for answers [...] that sort of radicalization was oriented toward education, public institutions. And as oftentimes happens in moral panics in this country and elsewhere, it's centered around children and their quote-unquote safety and what we think

should be and should not be sort of normative childhood development. When we say "normative childhood development" in this country, we mean white.

As a result of this radicalization, these outraged far-right parents organized themselves into groups like Moms for Liberty. As mask mandates expired, the groups began to seek other targets for their politics of outrage. They railed against what they called "critical race theory," a misapplied term that means, in their eyes at least, any discussion of race that casts a critical eye at systems like racial privilege. Then, they went after what they called "gender ideology," a made-up term that means (to them) any discussion of gender that makes space for queer, trans, and nonbinary people. They attacked children's rights to choose their own pronouns. They attacked trans people's rights to choose whatever bathroom best fit their identity. They attacked trans children's rights to play sports. In many cases, these attacks made it all the way into legislation, for instance Florida's 2022 Stop WOKE Act or restrictive bathroom bills in Kansas or Ohio. Representing a clear success of their goal to make local prejudice into national policy, on February 5, 2025, Donald Trump signed an executive order barring transgender athletes from participating on the sports teams that fit their gender.

At some point, the far right's so-called "anti-woke" crusade locked in on yet another target: books. Most often, books for children by queer authors or people of color. The school library became a battleground in a culture war, and many children and librarians became victims of a far-right assault on the right to read. The assault came in many forms, from library challenges, to intimidation, to actual legislation. The whole thing caused an atmosphere of fear that led to widespread soft censorship, wherein teachers and librarians take books off the shelves before they're even challenged, just to avoid the hassle and threats. Parallel to all this was a separate thread of anti-reading sentiment, directed at victims of political violence and colonization. It became very difficult, for instance, for Palestinian writers to have their voices heard amid Israel's massive assault after Hamas's October 7 attacks. It has also become nearly impossible to help prisoners access any books at all, let alone books that are relevant to their interests or identities. Until very recently, one jail only allowed one book: the Christian Bible. It is vital for us to track the American school and library anti-reading wave, which led to harassment, threats, and doxxing of librarians and booksellers. It is also important to track other anti-book threats, like Israel's targeting of Palestinian literary infrastructure or the systemic erasure of books and knowledge from America's prisons. A common thread unites all these stories: agitators from the political far right trying to limit vulnerable people's access to stories that represent them. As nationalism maintains its grip on countries like Israel and the United States, we must not let the freedom to read become a casualty.

AGAINST BOTHSIDESISM

A quick note that I don't want to write but I feel like I should: I refuse to "both sides" this issue. While there are arguments that some on the left are limiting free speech via so-called "cancel culture," nothing about "cancel culture" comes even close to the well-funded, organized, and ruthless free speech suppression of the far right. Any "both sides" argument crumbles under the fact that only one side of the political spectrum is harassing librarians, sending death threats to drag queens, passing anti-book legislation, or launching hostile takeovers of school boards with the expressed goal of destroying libraries from within. As Lyta Gold writes in *Dangerous Fictions*, cancel culture is like

> peewee football to the right wing's NFL. The conservative book bans have barred access to huge swaths of literature in libraries and school districts across the country, and

many librarians and school districts have been harassed and threatened, some to the point of quitting their jobs for their own safety. Meanwhile, in the worst version of left cancel culture, a handful of novelists have lost their book deals.[3]

Even if attempts to curtail free speech occur on all sides of the political spectrum, only the religious and fundamentalist right have launched a coordinated, well-funded, national movement with the aim of stripping books from the marginalized readers that need them the most. Of course, that doesn't mean the left is totally off the hook. In February 2025, the governor of deep-blue New York forced Hunter College to remove a job posting for a professorship in Palestinian Studies. Even in one of the country's bastions of liberalism, the religious right holds sway over what people can and can't say. The mere idea of the academic study of Palestinian history and culture was such an affront to the far-right Zionist interpretation of Judaism that the state government forced a state college to limit such speech. While cancel culture is a snowball fight compared to the right wing's all-out blitzkrieg, we must be careful that the left doesn't also start using legislation and political power to curtail access to certain stories. Curtailing the right to read is bad wherever it happens, and it's at its worst on the far right.

THE POWER OF BOOKS

A curious element of all this is the fact that this right-wing angst is directed at books. Book banners will falsely label a YA novel "pornography" and trip over themselves trying to ban it, all while the children they're claiming to protect can easily access a galaxy of actual pornography on their phones. In some ways, the desperation to ban books emphasizes books' power. But are books actually that powerful to the young mind in the 2020s? Lyta Gold writes, "Fictional stories have long been believed to have an uncanny power over hearts and minds, especially those of young people."[4] The power of fiction has always spooked certain people, from the Satanic Panic of the 1980s to Plato's assertion that anything but wholesome stories are unwelcome in his Republic. This power comes from fiction's ability to force us to engage with other people, a feat made more difficult in other forms of art. The fear of the other animates every moral panic, including this one, and goes a long way to explain that this is about more than just books. Indeed, as Gold writes,

> The panics over fiction are never fully *about* fiction; they're almost always deflections of some other, more formless anxiety. Anxiety about the body politic, anxiety about the next generation, anxiety about who gets to make and control art, anxiety about what kinds of people get to exist in the public imagination, and, at its deepest level, anxiety about what kinds of human activity can be categorized as valuable and therefore worthy of attention (and compensation) in the first place.[5]

This is clearly true of the current book ban crisis. To the far-right activists driving this attack on books, only their own Christian nationalist perspective deserves to exist. Any books or identities that fall outside that vision (or oppose that vision) must be erased. The anti-book movement will do whatever it takes to force their version of fundamentalist values onto the entire country, from banning books to eliminating public schooling altogether, which increasingly seems to be their endgame. When we're discussing book bans, we're really discussing the far right's attempt to eliminate thoughts and people that don't fit their narrow perspective; this includes honest discussion of racism, work to make schooling more inclusive, and trans people in general. This sense of ethnic nationalism isn't limited to America, either. The far-right Israeli government is launching horrifically violent attacks against the Palestinian people and their right to tell their own stories. This is nothing new; in fact, the idea of crushing Palestinian stories is as old (or older) than Israel itself, and the violent act of displacing Palestinians is intertwined with the destruction of Palestinian narratives. In 1984, Palestinian critic Edward Said wrote, "The 'idea' of a Palestinian homeland would have to be enabled by the prior acceptance of a narrative entailing a homeland. And this has been resisted as strenuously on the imaginative and ideological level as it has been politically."[6] So if banning books is really trying to ban ideas, perspectives, and people, then fighting book bans is also fighting for the beautiful, varied, and diverse world that exists outside of violent ethnic nationalist worldviews.

And there are many people fighting back. While the book banning movement is widespread, so is the resistance to it. Just as overwhelming as the torrents of news about attacks on books are the stories about people fighting back. Publishers, librarians, readers, students, and booksellers have seized the opportunity to resist the wave of anti-book activity. There's no way to tell all their stories in a single book; instead, I have chosen a few specific cases that are broadly representative of the fight for the freedom to read and the ways people can resist. There are publishers like City Lights and Beacon Press, giving voice to victims of genocide. There are folks resisting through the courts, like the Texas booksellers who sued to block book ban legislation. There are librarians and booksellers tirelessly working to distribute banned books to readers who need them. There are booksellers working to host inclusive programs even though their stores are receiving bomb threats. There are dedicated volunteers doggedly navigating a Kafkaesque bureaucracy to get books to incarcerated people. And there are people working to coordinate all those efforts through coalition building and sharing stories. Some of those stories are in this book; many others are out there in the world. As much as I'm frightened by the attack on books, I'm heartened by the growing number of people fighting back. Welcome to the resistance.

CHAPTER 1: HOWL AND THE ROOTS OF THE BOOK BAN CRISIS

"We have suffered too much in recent years from the clumsy antics of ignorant do-gooders." —*Howl and Other Poems*

SMALL BUT MIGHTY

To understand today's far-right assault on books, it is worthwhile to go back in time to another case of book banning. And so we start this book with the 1957 ban of Allen Ginsberg's *Howl and Other Poems*. In starting here, I hope to show that today's book ban crisis is a revved-up version of a decades-long attempt by the American far right to silence stories that challenge the status quo and, in doing so, silence their authors and readers. In this story we will also find a compelling portrait of an early crusader for the right to read. We have much to learn from how bookseller and publisher Lawrence Ferlinghetti handled the crisis.

As far as I can tell, the first indie bookstore banned books display was at San Francisco's City Lights Books in August 1957. Just four years old at that point, City Lights was a fraction of the size it is today (and even today, it's on the smaller side of iconic U.S. bookstores). Started by Lawrence Ferlinghetti and Peter Martin in June 1953, tiny City Lights began its life as America's first paperback-only bookstore. Now widely accepted, the paperback was then a new technology reserved for grocery-store checkout fare like romances and pulp novels. But as cutting-edge publishers like New Directions and Grove began publishing more literary titles in the paperback format, Ferlinghetti and Martin saw an opportunity to bring good literature to the masses at affordable prices in order to broaden the number of people who had access to quality writing. Ferlinghetti has explained that "one of the original ideas of the store was for it not to be an uptight place but a center for the intellectual community."[7] And so Ferlinghetti and Martin opened their paperbacks-only store to bring great literature to the masses in San Francisco's North Beach enclave, jammed between Chinese, Italian, and bohemian neighborhoods in the city's northeast sector. Soon after its founding, Peter Martin departed the venture, leaving Ferlinghetti as the sole proprietor of the small shop. Not too much later, City Lights became a hub for what would become a vital moment in American countercultural history. And Ferlinghetti was the reserved, quiet, benevolent figure orchestrating it all.

Despite its small stature, City Lights has always benefitted from huge window displays lining its hilly portion of Columbus Avenue. It was in one of these spacious windows that the first banned books display held court. The practice of banned books displays continues to this day, especially centered around Banned Books Week in October. Libraries and bookstores throw caution tape around their shelves and display books like those from City Lights's display, as well as contemporary targets like *Gender Queer* and Sarah Maas's steamy fantasies. But here's the important thing: While Ferlinghetti was stocking and maintaining his display of targeted books, he was also spearheading a court case that would shape the future of free speech in the United States. With one hand, he was selling thousands of copies of a poetry book called *Howl*. With his other hand, he was fighting for the right to publish cutting edge, boundary-pushing literature.

FAR-OUT POETS AND WANDERING INTELLECTUALS

Sometime in either late 1954[8] or early 1955,[9] a young Allen Ginsberg popped into City Lights to introduce himself to shop proprietor Lawrence Ferlinghetti. Though the bookstore was only a few years old, surely City Lights and Ferlinghetti had already gained enough of a reputation that an aspiring young poet like Ginsberg knew that it would behoove him to make himself known in the tiny triangle of paperbacks at Columbus and Broadway. At the advice of San Francisco poetry scene elder statesman Kenneth Rexroth, Ginsberg had brought along *Empty Mirror*, his manuscript of poems, in hopes that Ferlinghetti would want to publish it.[10] Ferlinghetti read Ginsberg's poems with interest but ultimately declined to publish them, in no small part because he didn't have the money to do so.[11] All was not lost, however: the two poets did strike up a friendship, united by an interest in poetry and politics. Very soon, Ferlinghetti would come to recognize Ginsberg as "another of those far-out poets and wandering intellectuals who had started hanging out" at the tiny North Beach bookstore.[12]

It was during this time that Ginsberg went on a fateful stroll. On October 17, 1954, Ginsberg took a significant amount of peyote and set off on foot in the San Francisco streets. Suffice to say, he did not enjoy himself. As part of his trip, Ginsberg hallucinated that the Saint Francis Drake Hotel had transformed into a child-eating demon that he named Moloch.[13] He wrote down the vision, which ended up recalling his other preoccupations and fears: his longing for his friend and sometime-lover Neal Cassady; his recent stint in a mental hospital, where he heard his friend and fellow inmate Carl Solomon's screams during electroshock treatments; his own mother, also institutionalized; the general decay of a stultifying American culture eating away at his friends and fellow writers. Throughout 1955, all this fear and energy and outrage found an outlet in a breathless, four-part, run-on poem that Ginsberg was calling "Howl for Carl Solomon." Ginsberg had the feeling he was onto something, and he wasn't alone. After reading an early draft that Ginsberg had mailed to him, Jack Kerouac wrote back, "Your HOWL FOR CARL SOLOMON is very powerful."[14]

And so, the poem, and Ginsberg, were headed in a promising direction. The poem didn't become a frenzy, though, until its first public reading. That now-legendary event happened on October 7, 1955, at 3119 Fillmore St. in San Francisco. Ginsberg, in those days ever the hustler, worked tirelessly to organize an event called "Six Poets at Six Gallery." He printed hundreds of fliers, placing them in every relevant bar and hangout in North Beach, including of course City Lights.

On the fateful night of the reading, Lawrence Ferlinghetti himself was in the packed-house crowd. The scene inside the reading was raucous. Ginsberg was the first to read after the intermission. He made his way uneasily to the stage and then uttered the poem's famous first line: "I saw the best minds of my generation destroyed by madness, starving, hysterical, naked." From there, Ginsberg's performance grew more and more passionate, more ecstatic trance than poem recitation. Not everyone was thrilled by the performance. Ruth Witt-Diamant, the founder of the San Francisco Poetry Center and a regular sponsor of Gallery Six's poetry readings, was taken aback by the poem's explicit language: "She thought that "such 'obscene' words at a general public performance, not to mention the open drinking, all in the presence of minors, could well bring down the law."[15] She unsuccessfully tried to coax host Kenneth Rexroth to cut Ginsberg off. Her reaction proved prescient.

Throughout the evening, Lawrence Ferlinghetti sat at the back of the room, quietly taking in the hysteria and intensity. He, along with nearly everyone there, seemed to know that something important had happened. From the stage, Rexroth had said, "This poem will make you famous from bridge to bridge."[16] Michael McClure later said that they all knew "at the deepest level that a barrier had been broken."[17] Ferlinghetti felt it too. Again, there is debate and conjecture about what happened next, but the widely accepted legend goes like this: Rather than congratulate him in person next time they saw each other, Ferlinghetti sat down to send Ginsberg a telegram. The telegram paraphrased a message that Ralph Waldo Emerson sent Walt Whitman exactly one hundred years before, when Emerson first read Whitman's *Leaves of Grass*. Ferlinghetti wrote to Ginsberg, "I greet you at the beginning of a great career. When do I get the manuscript?"[18]

TO PUBLISH AND TO FIGHT

Howl and Other Poems was eventually released as City Lights Pocket Poets Series #4 on November 1, 1956. Before he could do that, though, Ferlinghetti had a phone call to make. He knew that the poem he was bringing into the world was not only paradigm-shifting but also remarkably frank in its language. To paint its portrait of a depraved world, "Howl" employed words and phrases that some would consider obscene. So, Ferlinghetti got on the phone with the American Civil Liberties Union, commonly known as the ACLU. According to lawyer-authors Ronald K.L. Collins and David M. Skover, "Lawrence Ferlinghetti had foresight. Much as he liked 'Howl,' and ready as he was to publish it, he was not unmindful of the risks associated with publishing a work with colorful and homoerotic words."[19] If you asked Ferlinghetti, there was more at stake than just the fourth entry in his already-legendary Pocket Poets series. The way he saw it, an expensive legal battle could spell the premature demise of everything City Lights. The whole thing ran on a shoestring—we're talking about a three-hundred-square-foot bohemian bookstore that only sold inexpensive paperbacks. Ferlinghetti ended up talking to the ACLU's Lawrence Speiser, who said the ACLU would be happy to defend City Lights in case any legal trouble popped up around the poem's publication. Ginsberg was not only delighted by the arrangement but also by the prospect of a rabble-rousing legal fight. He wrote to his father, "I am almost ready to tackle the U.S. Govt out of sheer self delight. There is really a great stupid conspiracy of unconscious negative inertia to keep people from 'expressing' themselves."[20]

The publishing and the fight were intertwined from the get-go. According to one longtime City Lights personality, the question of defending the book arose at the exact same time as the question of publishing it. Paul Yamazaki, head buyer at City Lights for more than 50 years, tells me that "almost immediately after [Ferlinghetti] sends the telegram to Allen, he starts having conversations with the ACLU. He was really clear about the challenge that he was embarking from. And even before the phone call, he understood the broad dimensions of not just the literary understandings of what Allen was doing or attempting to do," but also the broader implications of publishing something like it. The fight to publish *Howl and Other Poems* was not sprung on Ferlinghetti, Ginsberg, and company. They knew what they were doing, and they were prepared for whenever trouble would arrive.

And arrive it did, of course. Once *Howl and Other Poems* was completed, revised, and ready to print, Ferlinghetti enlisted London's Villiers print shop to create the first printing of one thousand copies. Reputationally, Villiers was known to do a good job with saddle-stitched, letterpress poetry books like the Pocket Poets Series. But they were a bit squeamish about *Howl*'s contents, in no small part because of past trouble in the Bay Area. Because Villiers had had a run-in with San Francisco customs concerning a magazine called *Miscellaneous Man*, they insisted on putting asterisks in place of certain four-letter words.[21] Thus modified, the first printing of *Howl* was created and made it through customs undisturbed for its November 1 release date, which happened to ride a crest of good press about the poetry scene in San Francisco. The wave of excitement, with the eyes of the nation for the first time turning towards the Bay and its Beats, made quick work of the first printing of *Howl* and necessitated a second. It was that shipment that caused San Francisco Collector of Customs Chester McPhee to seize 520 copies of *Howl and Other Poems* on the grounds that the book was obscene, and that "you wouldn't want your children to come across it."[22] Though McPhee didn't even manage to seize the entire shipment from Villiers—one thousand copies slipped through his grip unnoticed—the fight for *Howl*, and free speech in America, was officially on.

THE FIGHT IS ON

Ferlinghetti and his allies sprang into action. Within days, the ACLU told McPhee that it would be contesting the legality of the seizure, "on the grounds that the book is not obscene."[23] The next month, Ferlinghetti, ever the bookseller attuned to what any publicity can do to book sales, ordered a 2,500-copy printing of *Howl and Other Poems* to be printed via mimeograph in the United States, thus circumventing U.S. Customs altogether. Letters to the editor flooded the *San Francisco Chronicle*, many in praise of *Howl* and Ferlinghetti's decision to publish it. One person writes that "the major principle involved is whether a collector of customs is a suitable person to select the reading material of the general public [...] We have suffered too much in recent years from the clumsy antics of ignorant do-gooders."[24] Another asks,

> Yet who are these guardians of our moral and political outlook? They do not possess any degrees in art nor any broad political worldviews that would enable them to say what people should read or think in our world, where new standards are being established...and moss-grown ethics

are being discarded. Must our America be censorship by the ninnies of the San Francisco customs house?[25]

Even more galvanizing support came from *Chronicle* columnist Abe Mellinkoff, who wrote, "The collector has no duty to protect my children . . . if he is going to pick up everything that is a menace to them, he is going to be confiscating night and day."[26]

On May 19, *Chronicle* book reviews editor William Hogan gave his entire *Between the Lines* column to Lawrence Ferlinghetti to defend *Howl* and its publication. Allen Ginsberg had earlier told Ferlinghetti to "prepare some sort of outraged and idiotic but dignified statement," and Ferlinghetti appears to have taken the advice to heart.[27] The bookseller-publisher opens the defiant piece by saying, "The San Francisco Collector of Customs deserves a world of thanks for seizing Allen Ginsberg's 'Howl and Other Poems' and thereby rendering it famous. Perhaps I could have a medal made. It would have taken years for critics to accomplish what the good collector did in a day, merely by calling the book obscene."[28] His refusal to be cowed is admirable, and perhaps a model for those facing book bans today.

Elsewhere in his May 1957 column, he writes, notably, that the poem "is a gestalt, an archetypal configuration of the mass culture which produced it. If it is also a condemnation of our official culture, if it is an unseemly voice of dissent, perhaps this is really why officials object to it." This is impossible to prove, of course. But, again and again in this book, we will see those in power attacking books that challenge the way of life they're trying to maintain. Under the guise of concern for children, authorities have long sought to limit control to books that question the status quo their authority seeks to maintain. *Howl* was not the first or last, but it is certainly an exemplar. Ferlinghetti knew the poem had teeth, and an increasing number of readers did, too. With a wave of public support and books flying out the door, Ferlinghetti was capitalizing on the book's publicity. The positive momentum continued when, on May 29, the U.S. Attorney in San Francisco dismissed the customs inspector's case, and the 520 captive copies were released. Despite the reprieve and the wave of good publicity, though, the trouble was far from over.

HOWL GOES TO TRIAL

Many of the copies of *Howl* that passed over the counter of City Lights in spring 1957 went through the hands of bookstore manager Shigeyoshi Murao. Long before Ferlinghetti was stoking a media circus about *Howl*, Murao was one of the beating hearts of the store, a quiet but constant bookselling fixture. He was the one working the register on June 3, 1957, when Russell Woods and Thomas Pagee bought one copy each of *Howl* and *Miscellaneous Man*. Woods and Pagee were undercover inspectors working for Captain William A. Hanrahan of the San Francisco Police Department's Juvenile Bureau.[29] Hanrahan was "a zealous smut hunter"; in fact, he "publicly announced that *Howl* would open the door for a host of book seizures he wanted to initiate."[30] So the stakes were already high: for this zealot cop, *Howl* was just a test case for a planned wave of book bans. Two weeks after they made their purchase, Woods and Pagee returned and arrested Murao, charging him with the "willful and lewd" sale of "obscene and indecent" materials.[31] Though the Hall of Justice was only three blocks away, Woods and Pagee made a show of driving Murao there in a squad car. At the time, Ferlinghetti was relaxing in Big Sur. A separate warrant was issued for him on the same charges, with the addition of the publication of said materials in violation of section 311.3 of the California Penal Code. *Howl* was officially on trial.

The outrage was immediate. The *Chronicle* published an editorial called "Making a Clown of San Francisco" that claimed, "The Police department [...has] contrived to give the community an appearance of profoundest imbecility" because "henceforth the legality of books will be measured with a kindergarten or grammar-school yardstick."[32] They also ran an editorial cartoon depicting two cops, one tossing a bookseller into a paddy wagon and one nailing a piece of paper onto the bookstore door proclaiming "HANRAHAN'S LAW: ALL BOOKS MUST BE FIT FOR CHILDREN TO READ."[33] Captain William A. Hanrahan is just one part of a long line of potential censors trying to bludgeon free expression under the deceptive guise of protecting children. To trot children's delicate sensibility into matters of free speech is to manufacture outrage against the literature in question, and that's exactly what Hanrahan was attempting. Shortly after the arrest, Hanrahan not only declared that *Howl* was "not fit for children to read," but also that "anything not suitable for publication in newspapers shouldn't be published at all."[34]

Of course, that's a remarkably narrow, reductive view of literature, and dangerous too. As William Hogan wrote in the *Chronicle* two days after Murao's arrest, "the raiding of bookstores on such a slim pretext is dangerous, to say nothing of a stupid, precedent. I think an enlightened American community is in bad trouble if it permits this example of thought control to continue." Hogan is right—the idea that a cop can march into a bookstore and arrest a bookseller based on the presumed content of the books in the store is absolutely a dangerous idea, and one worth resisting. Don't get comfortable, contemporary reader: the idea of criminal action against those who provide access to books is in vogue among the far right today. Introduced or enacted laws in Missouri, Arkansas, and elsewhere seek to criminalize librarians who shelve titles the state or its actors deem inappropriate for children. The battle that Ferlinghetti, Murao, and Ginsberg were embarking on was certainly high stakes and had a tremendous impact on the future of bookselling and publishing in the United States.

Good thing Ferlinghetti had already alerted the ACLU about the potential for exactly what ended up happening. They were ready to assemble a crack team of top lawyers to defend the tiny book: in fact, the amount of legal talent assembled by the ACLU showed exactly how much they saw riding on this case. It wasn't just about Ferlinghetti's right to publish the word "cock" or "fuck." After all, *Howl* was an incendiary text for reasons far beyond its cuss words. The poem's power only comes in part from its frank depictions of sexuality; *Howl*'s engine also runs on its outraged wail decrying the dominant and repressive status quo of 1950s America. Indeed, according to Collins and Skover, the battle at hand "was not merely over some 'dirty' words in litera-ture, but over competing visions of the nation: the perspective of an Eisenhower-like America that many held dear versus that of a Whitman-like America that the Beats cherished."[35] Though obscenity trials had happened over and over again since the in-vention of print, this was one of the first times where someone like Hanrahan could be seen as fighting against the headwinds of cultural change in order to preserve an outdated, repressive vision of America. As Collins and Skover put it, "What was at stake was the right to *dissent*."[36] In that way, the *Howl* trial is a lot like what's happening today. In 1957, far-right government and para-government actors were going against communism and anti-establishment dissent. Today they're going after sexual and racial identities that fall outside their narrow moralistic view of America. Two different fronts in the same war.

THE SUNDAY SCHOOL TEACHER, THE BUMBLING PROSECUTOR, AND THE READY DEFENSE

With all that in mind, you would not believe who was assigned to judge this thing. The Honorable Clayton M. Horn was a Sunday school Bible teacher. He was "a man who cared about the moral character of his world and those in it."[37] He believed "God was in the letter of the law."[38] This is how pious and conservative he was: just a few weeks before the *Howl* case landed on his docket, he was overseeing the trial of five young women accused of shoplifting. All five were found guilty. Their sentence? To go to a movie theater and sit through all 219 minutes of Charlton Heston's *The Ten Commandments.* After viewing the film, they were to write essays about its moral lessons. The whole thing turned into enough of a kerfuffle that Horn got the *Chronicle* editorial cartoon treatment, with the stuffy judge decked in Moses robes holding a tablet that declared "THOU SHALT NOT MISS *THE TEN COMMANDMENTS.*"[39] At the ACLU's advice, Ferlinghetti had already agreed to waive a jury trial, meaning the fate of *Howl* (and perhaps dissident publishing in general) lay in the hands of this one tightly-wound Sunday school teacher.

Regardless, the ACLU legal team was undaunted. They had a clear strategy and, once the trial started in August 1957, they executed it to perfection. Their aim was "to substantiate that *Howl* had serious literary value and did not primarily appeal to 'prurient' interests."[40] Their opponent in this task was Ralph McIntosh, a veteran prosecutor who nonetheless had little experience in constitutional questions of free speech. He did have a reputation for being "tough on smut," a reputation he'd bank on during the trial.[41] However, he was not a reader of poetry. This was apparent in his trial arguing, which amounted to throwing up his hands and saying, "Who understands this weird stuff anyway?" Many of his questions for the defense witnesses centered on isolating certain passages to highlight their alleged obscenity and put on an air of incomprehension. This, of course, is a tried-and-true strategy of book banners in widespread use today. As McIntosh was entering *Howl and Other Poems* into evidence, he read out loud the dedication page, which states, "All these books are published in heaven." McIntosh immediately followed that up by saying "I don't quite understand that, but let the record show, your honor, it's published by City Lights Pocketbook Shop."[42] During his closing arguments, McIntosh reiterated that "I don't understand it very well."[43]

One of McIntosh's main witnesses, aside from one of the arresting officers, was Gail Potter. As she took the stand, she somewhat strangely bragged that one of her literary bona fides was that she had "rewritten *Faust*."[44] The courtroom erupted in laughter. Later accounts of the trial call Potter anything from "somewhat embarrassing" to the trial's "comic relief."[45,46] But I hesitate to laugh off Gail Potter because she was attempting to deploy a cynical, dangerous argument that's used by aspiring book banners to this day: from the stand, Potter said, "Every great piece of literature, anything that can really be classified as literature, is of some moral greatness, and I think [*Howl*] fails to the *n*th degree."[47] Literature, according to this line of thought, must make some kind of positive moral argument; there is no room for characters or writing that represent dissenting views or complex morality. This is a dangerous lens through which to view literature, and it shows up on both the left and right today (though the right is much more fanatical and ruthless in applying it). It's a narrow, reductive view of art that robs authors of the ability to create anything more nuanced or complicated than a fable for children. It also denies literature the right to exist as art; under Potter's view, every novel had to be a moralistic fable. Despite its misunderstanding of art in general, the idea was out in the open in that San Francisco courtroom just as it is in school board meetings, libraries, and Goodreads pages today.

One of Prosecutor McIntosh's arguments claimed that if a bookseller is selling a lewd book, he must know that it is lewd, thus proving lewd intent.[48] The idea that every bookseller knows the level of spiciness in every book in their store, though ridiculous, also shows up today. Texas's 2023 book ban bill, HB 900, requires bookstores to grade the appropriateness of every book they've ever sold (and ever will sell) to a school. Much space will be devoted to HB 900 later in this book, but suffice to say, this is yet another idea from the *Howl* trial that didn't end with the judge's ruling. Much to the relief of Shigeyoshi Murao, this idea was also viewed skeptically by Judge Horn. Early in the trial, Judge Horn determined that "there is nothing in the record showing that [Murao] has read these books, or knew their contents, or that there was any lewd intent in his part in selling them."[49] On August 22, charges against Murao were dropped.

Murao was one in a long line of booksellers residing in an uncomfortable position in the realm of activist bookselling: What happens when the advocacy and actions of a bookstore's higher-ups mean that the consequences of those actions fall on the booksellers themselves? While Ferlinghetti had well-documented and noble aspirations to defend the freedom of the press, Murao was in a much more uncomfortable spot. He has said, "In jail, I had no noble thoughts for fighting for freedom of the press . . . I had planned to live a quiet life of reading, listening to music and playing chess the rest of my life. Yet here I was involved in a case for selling obscenity."[50] Even worse, while privileged white dissident Ferlinghetti could wear a mugshot as a point of pride, being arrested meant something different in Murao's family. Ferlinghetti himself has said that "to be arrested for anything, even if innocent, was in the Japanese community of that time a family disgrace."[51] Even though Murao emerged without a conviction, the whole ordeal must have been painful for him. He'd go on to work at City Lights for almost two more decades before departing in a falling-out with Ferlinghetti.

The dismissal of Murao's charges was a blow to the prosecution. Even worse for the prosecution was the defense team's preparedness and thoroughness in arguing their case. To start, Judge Horn was well aware of the new precedent set by a recent case named *Roth v. United States,* which clarified the government's definition of obscenity. The end result of *Roth* was Justice William J. Brennan, Jr.'s four-way obscenity test: "Whether to the average person, applying contemporary community standards, the dominant theme of the material taken as a whole appeals to prurient interest."[52] Judge Horn even said so from the bench, claiming, "This Court feels that it will follow the *Roth* decision as the basis of what may or may not be the subject of an exclusion or exception to the First Amendment."[53] Therefore, in theory, all the defense had to do was prove that *Howl and Other Poems,* as a whole, had some literary merit. To start, ACLU lawyer J.W. Erlich argued that "individual words in and of themselves do not make obscene books [...] Some people think that certain four-letter words in and of themselves destroy mankind from a moral standpoint. This, of course, is not the law."[54]

Prosecutor McIntosh had somehow missed this memo, as part of his strategy was to read choice juicy portions of *Howl* out loud to enter them into the record: "The prosecutor repeated again and again—indeed no fewer than 24 times—the very four-letter, and five-, six-, seven-, and eight-letter words that he deemed "obscene" terms violating the California penal law."[55] Again, though, lest you dismiss this strategy of picking individual passages with bad words as silly or outdated, consider the myriad school board meetings at this very moment where angered parents are doing just that with books like *Gender Queer.* Some people willfully ignore the "taken as a whole" part of the *Roth* test. But would Judge Horn?

Once the defense argued that individual words or passages were not enough to deem a whole work obscene, the next question was that of *Howl's* literary merit. On September 5, 1957, a parade of nine literary experts argued just that. One of the experts testifying to the literary merit of *Howl* was none other than Kenneth Rexroth. One must wonder if Rexroth imagined this scene while he lorded over the delirious and exciting Six Gallery reading. Regardless, he was more than up to the task, claiming that "the simplest term for such writing [as *Howl*] is prophetic . . . the theme is the denunciation of evil and a pointing of the way out, so to speak. That is prophetic literature."[56] Another effective witness was *San Francisco Examiner* book editor Luther Nichols, who claimed,

> Mr. Ginsberg is expressing his personal view of a segment of life that he has experienced. It is a vagabond one; it's colored by exposure to Jazz, to Columbia, a university, to a liberal and bohemian education, to a great deal of traveling on the road, to a certain amount of what we call bumming around. He has seen in that experience things that do not agree with him, that have perhaps embittered him. He has also seen things at a social level concerned with the atom bomb, and the materialism of our time. In sum, I think it's a howl of pain.[57]

In whole, the series of witnesses made a forceful argument for the literary merit of *Howl*. This despite the fact that Ferlinghetti, Murao, and Ginsberg weren't called as witnesses (Ginsberg wasn't even in the country at the time). All the defense had to do was prove that the book was not obscene; reading the trial transcripts, it seems like they were not only doing that but trying to prove that it was great literature.

On top of the parade of expert witnesses giving well-articulated defenses of *Howl*'s literary merit, young ACLU lawyer Albert M. Bendich prepared "A Memorandum of Points and Authorities" for Judge Horn's consideration. The document ended up being just as persuasive as anything else in the defense's playbook, a concise and methodical explanation of the ACLU's legal argument.

Well-supported by precedent and research, the document argued that "the fundamental freedoms of speech and press [...]

prohibited the suppression of any literature by application of the obscenity test unless the trial court first determined that the work was utterly without socially redeeming value."[58] Bendich's arguments were so persuasive that Judge Horn's eventual decision essentially paraphrased large portions of it.

"I FIND THE BOOK IS NOT OBSCENE."

A month after the conclusion of the trial's arguments, Judge Horn took the unusual step of issuing a written opinion for a municipal court case. There was no room for doubt here, with Horn writing, "I conclude the book *Howl and Other Poems* does have some redeeming social importance, and I find the book is not obscene."[59] Judge Horn arrived at this conclusion thanks to a 12-point test of his devising, which I'll quote in full here simply because the ruling continues to shape free speech debates to this day:

1. If the material has the slightest redeeming social importance it is not obscene because it is protected by the First and Fourteenth Amendments of the United States Constitution, and the California Constitution.

2. If it does not have the slightest redeeming social importance it may be obscene.

3. The test of obscenity in California is that the material must have a tendency to deprave or corrupt readers by exciting lascivious thoughts or arousing lustful desire to the point that it presents a clear and present danger of inciting to anti-social or immoral action.

4. The book or material must be judged as a whole by its effect on the average adult in the community.

5. If the material is objectionable only because of coarse and vulgar language which is not erotic or aphrodisiac in character it is not obscene.

6. Scienter [intent to harm or cause damage] must be proved.

7. Book reviews may be received in evidence if properly authenticated.

8. Evidence of expert witnesses in the literary field is proper.

9. Comparison of the material with other similar material previously adjudicated is proper.

10. The people owe a duty to themselves and to each other to preserve and protect their constitutional freedoms from any encroachment by government unless it appears that the allowable limits of such protection have been breached, and then to take only such action as will heal the breach.

11. I agree with Mr. Justice Douglas: I have the same confidence in the ability of our people to reject noxious literature as I have in their capacity to sort out the true from the false in theology, economics, politics, or any other field.

12. In considering material claimed to be obscene it is well to remember the motto: "Honi soit qui mal y pense." (Evil to him who evil thinks.)[60]

The ruling is remarkable in its scope and its creation of space for boundary-pushing literature. Where some would ban books because of single passages with sexual content (and the world is crawling with these folks to this day), Judge Horn's decision requires nuance and the judging of an entire work before it can be deemed obscene. Any work that can be reasonably proven to have even a shred of social merit—by book reviews, by experts, by comparison to other works—is protected by the First Amendment. The decision's legacy persists to this day: It "set in motion a new era in press and poetic freedom. Though that precedent never found its way onto the pages of the *Supreme Court Reports*, it did, nonetheless, weave its way into the quilt of the American culture."[61] And so a Sunday school teacher with a penchant for Charlton Heston, in a municipal court usually reserved for traffic tickets, made a forceful decision to defend free speech, shaping American freedom for the rest of the twentieth century and beyond.

REVOLUTIONARY LITERATURE AND THOSE WHO MAKE IT POSSIBLE

No single person successfully defended *Howl* on their own. The salvation of the book from the grasps of Captain Hanrahan and his team of would-be book banners was a team effort. Just ask Nancy Peters, Ferlinghetti's eventual business partner at City Lights: "Sometimes nobody speaks up, and the banned book stays banned. For better or worse, the legal system depends on and is shaped by citizen involvement."[62] Or, as Collins and Skover put it,

> Think of it all from a First Amendment perspective: a poet dared to write a poem condemning the guardians of the societal canon, a publisher dared to print that poem, a bookseller dared to sell and circulate that poem and then defend it in court, a newspaper dared to rally to the cause of the poet, publisher, and bookseller, and finally a god-fearing judge dared to protect the poem and the publisher in the name of the law.

Many people played a role in the defense of *Howl* as a community of readers, booksellers, publishers, and writers came to its defense (and, by extension, to the defense of the freedom of speech). Of course, Lawrence Ferlinghetti was the face of this effort. He chose to publish the book, yes, recognizing its revolutionary potential and its importance to American literature in general. At every point, he showed a canny awareness of the importance of what he was doing. As soon as he decided to publish the book, he was on the phone with the ACLU to prepare for any eventual trouble, a move that proved prescient. When part of the second shipment from England was seized by San Francisco Customs, he found a way to print more in America. Despite his shy and reserved nature, he was defiant and outspoken at every opportunity. He filled his front window with what could've been the first-ever banned books display. He issued a defiant rallying cry in the pages of the *Chronicle*. It's worth a pause here to reflect on the role of the *Chronicle* and other newspapers in all this—today, as local newspapers and newspaper book sections disappear into a Facebook- and AI-powered media Moloch, it's hard to imagine a character like a newspaper book review editor playing such a major role in a national censorship controversy. But that's exactly what happened when William Hogan handed over his column so Ferlinghetti could wax defiant on newsprint. Hogan's interest in the case combined with Ferlinghetti's defiance combined to form a winning strategy in the battle to defend Ginsberg's iconoclastic, revolutionary poem.

But Ferlinghetti didn't act alone. For one thing, that phone call to the ACLU led to a prepared and persuasive team of lawyers that covered every angle of the case, from preparing the witnesses to make strong testimony, to knowing the relevant case law and convincing the judge to follow it, to winning over the audience and the broader population with courtroom charisma. But even beyond that, much of the San Francisco community pitched in to make sure *Howl* could sound its barbaric yawp undeterred. Other bookstores even chipped in, a clear model for how they can help with today's assault on freedom of expression. Immediately before the trial began, 21 San Francisco bookstores sent a letter to the mayor calling for an end to the police seizure of books and protesting the arrests of Ferlinghetti and Murao. Two booksellers were on trial, and the petition to the mayor was a meaningful show of solidarity with lessons for today's climate. Indeed, whether he knew it or not, Shig Murao was putting a lot on the line to be able to sell *Howl*. He paid a personal cost for the sake of literature, an uncomfortable truth about what sometimes needs to happen to make groundbreaking literature available to the masses.

But beyond the risk and the political declarations, at the heart of the controversy was a tiny bookstore that was doing important work to become the nexus of a revolutionary literary community. That work was not without risks: Throughout the entire *Howl* saga, Ferlinghetti "became an example (albeit a rare one) of a fearless businessman who stood firmly and proudly on his rights. It is easy to overlook the fact that Ferlinghetti's stand could have gone south; he could have lost the case, his liberty, and his business. How many businesspeople would follow his example?"[63] The answer to that may hold a key to the free speech battles of today. Bookstores, publishers, and other businesses hold tremendous power and potential to fight off the current generation of book banners. After all, City Lights the bookstore went a long way to foment the conditions that enabled Ginsberg to write his incendiary verse for City Lights the publisher. According to Beat Generation biographer Bill Morgan, "City Lights was one of the first bookstores in the county to encourage readers to linger in the store and read the books. They provided chairs to relax on. As a result, the store became headquarters for the literary community of North Beach."[64] Sometimes it's as simple as that: before he became Ginsberg's publisher, Ferlinghetti, via his bookstore, was the custodian of a place where Ginsberg could hang out and meet likeminded writers. Without the fearless backing of Ferlinghetti and the community surrounding his bookstore, *Howl* might have never happened.

In conclusion, it's worth wondering why exactly Hanrahan and others made a run at *Howl*, of all books. It was a tiny pamphlet of poetry published by a tiny bookstore; surely there were more prurient and more widely distributed books. After all, Ferlinghetti is correct in asserting that the trial was what made *Howl* a bestseller, and eventually a legendary, canonical book. There's a parallel universe somewhere where *Howl* was quietly read by a small cult of readers and then forgotten. So why *Howl*? Were a few curse words really enough to make Captain Hanrahan take a stand? There are some who believe not. Rather, some experts claim that the poem's revolutionary potential (which was enabled by Hanrahan's very efforts to quash it) made the authorities try to clamp down. According to Collins and Skover, "It wasn't just *Howl*'s colorful words, such as 'cock,' 'fucked,' and 'balled.' It was also the poem's aggressive and activist message, those tirades against McCarthy-era politics and Norman Rockwell-era morality. That message was far more threatening to the conventions of the day than any barroom vernacular."[65] Ginsberg himself felt like the issue was bigger than four-letter words, wondering in a letter to Ferlinghetti, "Who or what is behind all this attention?"[66] Ferlinghetti was suspicious as well, writing in the *Chronicle* that *Howl* "is a gestalt, an archetypal configuration of the mass culture which produced it. If it is also a condemnation of our official culture, if it is an unseemly voice of dissent, perhaps this is really why officials object to it."[67] Something like this is impossible to prove, of course, especially since those arguing that *Howl* was obscene were so sloppy and scattershot in their arguments. But Ginsberg's opus *did* shake up the culture, an early salvo in the revolution that would shift American popular culture away from the sanitized, McCarthyist 1950s towards the more radical 1960s.

As Ferlinghetti wrote on the occasion of *Howl*'s 50th anniversary, "*Howl* became the catalyst in a paradigm shift in American poetry and consciousness. The Beats were advance word slingers prefiguring the counterculture of the 1960s, forecasting its main obsessions and ecstasies of liberation."[68] Only speculation could tell us whether that paradigm shift would've happened the same way if Captain Hanrahan hadn't gone after *Howl*. But evidence of the rift remains today. There are those who still attack books that question the dominant norms and forces of what the far right considers American culture. And there are those in power who attempt to wield that power to take us back to the pre-*Howl* era of what Ferlinghetti calls "repressive, conformist, racist, homophobic" American morality.[69] There are people who claim that any mention of sexuality makes a book pornographic. There are people who highlight single passages containing colorful language and claim those individual sentences make a whole book obscene. There are people who ignore the long precedent of free speech case law, upon which Judge Horn had such a huge impact. This is why I open this book with an in-depth investigation into the fight over *Howl*: the fight is still raging today, and we'll need a lot more Lawrence Ferlinghettis if we're going to win.

Of course, this is all on current City Lights steward Elaine Katzenberger's mind. She's well aware of how today's climate mirrors the McCarthyism that led to the attack on *Howl*. Katzenberger tells me that the hostile climate for libraries in the United States is

> just continuing and it's worse. I mean, they're passing all of these laws now and institutionalizing this state by state where they can, and that's going to be a fight to undo. And also look what's happening to the American Library Association and the entire public notion of libraries themselves and whether or not they have value or whether they're a threat to your community. Those kinds of things are really, really dangerous. And I think it's strange that [...] it's a relatively quiet thing as far as the alarms that should be going off for everyone, especially anybody who has kids. Because the target, of course, is the kids. That's the excuse for all of this. And it's all about making sure that their young minds are not exposed to whatever ideas that people find offensive or potentially dangerous.

Katzenberger is right: there is a war on free expression happening right now in the United States, and libraries aren't just on the front lines; they *are* the front lines.

☞ HOW TO DEFEND BOOKS

BE PROACTIVE, NOT REACTIVE

At no point during the *Howl* brouhaha was Ferlinghetti caught off guard. He knew what kind of book he had, and he knew all about the forces that could fight against it. So, at the same time as he was finalizing the book for publication, he was in contact with the ACLU. Because of this, at the first sign of trouble, the ACLU had a strategy and a team of lawyers ready to fight. Today's publishers would be well-suited to practice this preparedness instead of playing catch-up to the well-organized and seemingly tireless book ban movement. Publishers can prepare a legal strategy and lawyer up, so they're prepared if book banners come for one of their titles. Authors can join networks with other authors, such as Authors Against Book Bans, to share strategies and solidarity in case of a ban attack. Readers can familiarize themselves with curation policies at their local schools in libraries, the better to defend such institutions against attacks.

DO NOT SHRINK AWAY

Book bans are not popular, and they regularly poll poorly. On top of this, the book banning strategies employed by the far right—yelling at teenagers, reading dirty words in city council meetings, calling non-pornographic books "porn" at a time when actual porn is more available than it's ever been in human history—are all kind of ridiculous. The irascible Ferlinghetti was defiant and hilarious through the whole thing. Never a craven capitalist, Ferlinghetti kept focus on how the trial was selling books, not to brag but to take wind out of the book banner's sails. Book ban resistance fighters could stand to use more irreverence and defiance to show we are not cowed by the far right's fear tactics. As scary as a ban attack can be, if possible, authors and readers should go on offense about book banning tactics. Why exactly does this person spend all day trawling school library databases for books about trans people? How can this person show their face in public after berating a 14-year-old at a city council meeting? What's so scary about two male penguins raising a baby penguin together? Right wingers have made great hay of the idea of a "liberal snowflake," but if they can't handle the idea of *And Tango Makes Three*, who's the real snowflake? Rather than go on defense (which is what they want you to do—they want to make it seem like you're defending children accessing pornography), go on offense. I will add one caveat to this: The trial impacted Lawrence Ferlinghetti and Shig Murao in different ways, in large part due to cultural differences and levels of privilege. Make sure being feisty won't put anyone in danger, especially when threats are involved. In some cases, it may be more prudent to avoid escalating a situation. Tread carefully, and if your level of privilege allows you to do it, get feisty.

USE THE PRESS

In retrospect, it's pretty wild to see the role the *Chronicle* played in this story, from editorials to cartoons to lending column space to Ferlinghetti himself. Sadly, this is likely possible because of the role of newspapers in public life in 1957, a role almost entirely diminished today. Though newspapers aren't really it anymore, there are still media that people turn to, and book ban fighters can use that media as an ally. Find a sympathetic platform with a big audience and take your pro-book argument there. Book banners have found lots of ways to amplify their voices, despite the unpopularity of their mission. Book ban resisters can do the same thing, with potentially greater reach since most people agree with us. Several anti- book ban organizations have large social media followings. Popular Substack newsletter authors like Maris Kreizman write frequently and well about the crisis. Some media outlets, like *LitHub* and *BookRiot*, still do cover the book ban crisis on a regular basis. Additionally, short form video platforms like Instagram Reels and TikTok are full of readers who believe in the freedom to read. Don't underestimate the potential for your message to resonate there.

CHAPTER 2 : SCHOOLS AND LIBRARIES ON THE FRONT LINES

"No 17-year-old should have been put through any of that."
—Cameron Samuels

*D*uring the 2023-2024 school year, 10,046 book ban attempts were reported to PEN America.[70] That's double the entire previous school year and triple the one before that. The ban attempts happened in 42 states, crossing any so-called "red state" / "blue state" divide. Those are shocking numbers already, even more so when one considers that 82-97 percent of book ban attempts go unreported and receive no media coverage.[71] That means the number of actual book ban attempts in the 2023-2024 school year could easily exceed 300,000. Statistically, that's more than two for every single school library and public library in the country. In nearly every reported case, the attempted book bans "target books about sexual violence and rape, books about LGBTQ+ identities and experiences, and books with characters of color or that explore themes of race and racism."[72] And that's just the actual, formal censorship attempts. This book banning movement has also created a climate of fear that has led to widespread soft censorship. For one thing, a climate of fear has impacted libraries' curation decisions. Librarians will choose a "safer" book, meaning a book that avoids discussion of race or LGBTQ+ identities, because it's less likely to cause trouble or threaten their job. On top of that, it's common for libraries to remove a book from the shelves, or otherwise restrict access, as soon as a challenge is recorded, regardless of the eventual outcome. In this way, a simple challenge turns into an automatic ban, even if there is no merit to the challenge itself. There are countless accounts of newly emboldened library or school administrators looking to remove books with no regard for existing reconsideration policies. One school librarian put it this way: "The last four years have demonstrated to me that superintendents or administrators often feel entitled to remove books from libraries because of their own particular sensitivities [. . .] in most cases, the only thing between *them* and the removal of that book is somebody like me—a librarian—who reminds them that, 'no, we have policies around this.'"[73] This is a vital role for a librarian to play: to keep hostile administrators in check. But, increasingly, burned-out librarians are leaving the profession to flee the newly hostile environment of a library under siege.

Throughout the chaos of the book ban movement, burned-out librarians have faced harassment, threats, and doxxing. This is all playing out against the backdrop of increasing demands on public libraries that had them stretched thin even before the book ban crisis roared to life. The disappearance of safe public spaces and the social safety net has meant that libraries are providing services once left to governments and agencies. Often, the library is the only place offering safe shelter, clean bathrooms, and even drinking water to transient or houseless citizens. That's not to mention access to the internet or printers or even phones. As Donald Trump and his ilk destroy the agencies providing public services, libraries have taken on the mantle of technological and financial literacy, all while facing catastrophic budget cuts. Still, school libraries, and the books they contain, may be the only safe place for a closeted queer student or a student exploring their identity. Poet Rupi Kaur, in reaction to her books being banned, posted on her Facebook page, "i remember sitting in my school library in high school, turning to books about sexual assault because i didn't have anyone else to turn to."[74] The books they access from the library could be the only place that a student sees their own identity reflected without any judgment or hostility. The books could also be the sole source of frank and honest discussion of sex. Multiple states have passed laws banning "instruction on 'gender identity, gender expression, or sexual orientation' in *any* grade."[75] A student might need library books to learn anything about sexuality or queer identity at all. Follow this logic, an attack on books becomes an attack on people, often highly vulnerable young queer people. Indeed, hate crimes against LGBTQ+ students have sharply risen in recent years, and the trend is most severe in states with anti-LGBTQ+ legislation.[76] I would argue that this is precisely what's going on: Those in power are trying to attack (or worse, eliminate) entire identities, and they're starting by trying to ban the books that depict those identities.

Follow any of these trends back to their origin, and you'll more than likely find yourself, if not in 1957 San Francisco, then in 2020 at the beginning of the Covid-19 pandemic. Go a step further, and you'll find yourself face to face with Moms for Liberty, one of the central villains in the entire book ban saga. The Moms for Liberty story begins in Brevard County, Florida, in August 2020. An election for a Brevard School District school board seat saw Jennifer Jenkins handily beat incumbent Tina Descovich. In Florida, school board elections are nonpartisan, though Jenkins clearly leans Democrat while Descovich is far-right MAGA. The race became a referendum on the raging Covid-19 pandemic; Jenkins campaigned on a message of prioritizing safety with cautious school reopenings and mask mandates. Descovich, on the other hand, fiercely opposed mask mandates and any kind of overarching government attempt at public health safety. Jenkins won handily despite Republican turnout being higher in the election.[77] The result left local Republicans reeling; Brevard Republican Executive Committee Chairman Rick Lacey went as far as to suggest Republicans accidentally voted for Jenkins.[78] Vehement anti-masker Tina Descovich was left wondering what to do.

Descovich and her team incorporated Moms for Liberty as a 501(c)(4) nonprofit on January 1, 2021. Less than a month later, Descovich was on the *Rush Limbaugh Show*. By the end of February 2021, the group had gotten attention from *Breitbart* and *Tucker Carlson Tonight*. To receive this much conservative media attention this quickly after being founded is remarkable, especially since Moms for Liberty didn't even have that many members. In fact, the right-wing media acted as a recruiter for the organization. As *Media Matters* puts it,

> What can't be emphasized enough is just how small Moms for Liberty was when major media attention began and how crucial that coverage was to the group's expansion, with influential right-wing media figures functionally recruiting their eager audience to join the organization. As media attention of the group increased, new chapters were created and more members joined.[79]

Like Ferlinghetti before them, Moms for Liberty sought the media's help in spreading their message, except theirs was one of hate.

If you ask Descovich or any other member of Moms for Liberty, they'd say their message is simply "parents' rights," that the government shouldn't have more influence than parents over what children learn. But, as *Media Matters* puts it, "These well-connected partisans are opportunistically manufacturing outrage and selling it to parents under the guise of empowerment."[80] It all started with mask mandates and spread from there. The Moms for Liberty T-shirts—the shirts that allegedly pay for all their operations—say, "We do not co-parent with the government." According to the Southern Poverty Law Center, what's actually happening is that "Moms for Liberty commonly propagates conspiracy theories about public schools attempting to indoctrinate and sexualize children with a progressive Marxist curriculum."[81] Their answer to the so-called Marxist curriculum is to push for the elimination of the Department of Education altogether, a mission now embraced by none other than President Donald Trump and his wildly unqualified Secretary of Education Linda McMahon. Cementing the federalization of Moms for Liberty's homegrown philosophy is The America 250 Civics Education Coalition, a DoE-led initiative gathering more than forty far-right groups including the Heritage Foundation, PragerU, and Moms for Liberty themselves.

Of course, it's interesting that a group that's so opposed to public schools is spreading that message by trying to take over school boards and the Department of Education, but one tried-and-true political method of the far right is to take over an institution and destroy it from within. This school-board tactic isn't just tacit, it's official: Moms for Liberty has hosted trainings and provided resources explicitly designed to run a successful school board campaign. But their goal isn't to serve as effective stewards and leaders for the school districts of America; a much better key to understand Moms for Liberty and other groups like it is the idea of manufacturing outrage.

Even if their message is hateful, their tactics are perhaps even more so. Just ask Jennifer Jenkins, the Brevard, Florida, school board member who unseated Descovich. Close as it was to the heart of Mom's for Liberty's origins, Jenkins's district became a flashpoint. According to an op-ed Jenkins wrote for *The Washington Post*, one of her political opponents had falsely reported that she abused her daughter, sending an investigator from the Florida Department of Children and Families to Jenkins's house.[82] She has been called a Nazi, a pedophile, and threatened repeatedly.[83] Protesters showed up outside her house, shouting chants that accused Jenkins of pedophilia as her neighbors walked by. They confused friends on her porch for Jenkins herself, yelling at them that "we're coming at you like a freight train! We are going to make you beg for mercy. If you thought January 6 was bad, wait until you see what we have for you!"[84] Florida *state rep* Randy Fine posted Jenkins's private cell phone number on Facebook. Go back and read that last sentence again.

The sad thing is, Jennifer Jenkins is far from the only victim of these violent and hateful tactics. Even if these attacks weren't all launched by Moms for Liberty themselves, they certainly didn't denounce them, either. Moms for Liberty is instrumental in creating the climate that has invited such tactics into libraries, school board meetings, and homes across the country. And politicians are far from the only victims—don't forget the students themselves. Queer students, trying to find their way and see themselves in what they read, are now caught up in a political pissing match instigated and escalated by propaganda-spreading far-right conspiracy theorists.

The consequences could be severe. There's abundant evidence that book bans cause actual harm, and conversely, that environments without bans are better for students. *Scientific American* describes one study that observed four classrooms where students could freely choose whatever they wanted to read; in such classrooms, "The students talked to one another about themes in the books they read, developed compassion and empathy for the characters and their struggles, and thought about choices and consequences. In addition, their mental health improved."[85] The *Scientific American* op-ed goes on to claim that out-of-control book bans will create a generation of "young people who will not question authority, build alliances with people who have less political power, or challenge the status quo"—millions of children who "don't know what they don't know."[86] Some scientific research supports this; one study asserts that "banning books about the lived experiences and histories of marginalized groups of people only serve to increase feelings of exclusion and invisibility, and intensify their risk of mental health issues."[87] This impacts groups that are *already* disproportionately affected by mental health issues. It's well documented that queer people have much higher rates of suicide, and BIPOC people "are at a higher risk of facing mental health issues, and have increased barriers to accessing mental health treatment, due to institutional and interpersonal discrimination, stigma, and socioeconomic barriers."[88] In addition to mental health consequences, book bans have pedagogical impacts, too. Studies have found that removing access to books decreases connection amongst peers and increases student reliability on unreliable or misleading information.[89] Of course, book bans primarily impact already-marginalized students, but they're also bad for students in the majority. White students suffer by the removal of BIPOC books too, because research shows that "books about characters who are not like you are the best for building empathy."[90] The research is abundantly clear: Access to commonly challenged books is good for students, and banning those books is bad.

These books and readers must be defended and protected from this vicious right-wing assault. The best way to prepare this defense is to understand the tactics that Moms for Liberty and other anti-book crusaders are using. Once we understand their strategy, we can better develop ways to fight back.

HOW BOOK BANNERS DO IT: THE RIGHT WING'S STRATEGIES FOR DESTROYING THE RIGHT TO READ

CIRCULATE LISTS OF BOOKS TO BAN

The first decision that a potential book banner must make is which book to challenge or ban. Counter to any reasonable logic, the first step here is rarely to actually read a book or engage in honest and meaningful conversation with your child about what they're reading. It's much easier and faster for a list of books to tell you what to ban. In Texas, Rep. Matt Krause sent threatening letters to school superintendents, trying to force them to audit their collections for book appearing on a seemingly random list of 850 books. The chosen list for Moms for Liberty and their ilk was a now-defunct website called BookLooks.org. While it's no longer in operation, BookLooks managed to do a great deal of damage in its short life. Its mission, at least on its surface, claimed to be to "write and collect detailed and easy to understand book content reviews centered around objectionable content, including profanity, nudity, and sexual content. Our goal is to make these reviews available to all parents so they can make informed decisions."[91] The site even claimed, "We are not affiliated with any other groups, nor do we actively or materially support any groups," but that appears to be an outright lie. According to a 2022 *BookRiot* article, "BookLooks is spearheaded by Moms for Liberty member Emily Maikisch, per filings. The site uses the same rating system shared on the Moms for Liberty Brevard County public Facebook page, published in late March [2022]."[92] Moms for Liberty recruited volunteers to help generate the ratings and reviews on BookLooks. As *BookRiot* put it, "There is a direct link between Moms For Liberty and BookLooks."[93]

Having an in-house source of books deemed "obscene" by Moms for Liberty's restrictive and non-legally based definition of obscenity makes it easier for Moms for Liberty to file book challenges. It was a wildly efficient tool; in Carroll County, Maryland, alone, Moms for Liberty has challenged 50 books, all of which were found on BookLooks.[94] Nine were officially banned, the rest were likely subject to any number of types of soft censorship. BookLooks made this kind of challenge frictionless: simply browse their list of books (which, of course, isn't assembled by any kind of transparent methodology). Click on the title, and a ready-to-print PDF pops up with a detailed list of out-of-context passages, ready to read out loud (see the next section). For instance, the classic novel *Beloved* had a rating of 3, meaning "minor restricted." The PDF file for *Beloved* warned of "sexual activities; beastiality [sic] commentary; violence; racial commentary; profanity; and derogatory terms." Of course, a good-faith reader of this classic novel would think that racial commentary is perhaps the point. Another prizewinning classic, Alison Bechdel's comic memoir *Fun Home*, nabbed a 4, meaning "not for minors." Its BookLooks PDF warned of "alternate sexualities; alternate gender ideologies; profanity; alcohol use; suicide commentary; controversial religious commentary; sexual activities; and sexual nudity." This one even had images of the comic panels in question. One of the passages highlighted in the report, strangely, was the sentence, "There's no proof, actually, that my father killed himself." Also, "He thought that I thought that he was queer." Apparently, this was enough to count for pornography in the logic of Moms for Liberty. Of course, the packet also had a "profanity count:" "Bitch: 2; Fag/Faggot: 2; Fuck: 4; Homo: 1; Piss: 1; Shit: 3." It doesn't take an English grad student to say that counting cuss words and highlighting every instance of the word "queer" does not count as proper analysis of whether a work is obscene. The law agrees: widely accepted free speech case law demands consideration of the work as a whole.

Still, this didn't stop Moms for Liberty from developing the false, disingenuous, and misleading BookLooks tool. It also didn't stop its implementation from being successful until it was shut down without explanation in March 2025. While their reasons for 86ing Booklooks were mysterious, it is worth noting that, also in March 2025, eight families sued the St. Francis, Minnesota, school district over the district's use of BookLooks in curating their libraries. Though this particular tool is now gone, its resources surely exist in the digital ether. On top of that, its legacy of creating a sloppy canon of book ban targets lives on in the strategies and methodologies of book banners.

TAKE PASSAGES OUT OF CONTEXT

We saw it in the *Howl* trial, and we've seen it again and again since then: To rule whether something is pornographic or obscene, the cumulative effect of the entire work must be taken into consideration. Seventy years after the *Howl* verdict, there is abundant legal precedent that clearly asserts a work must be taken as a whole to determine whether its obscene or not. But school board members are not judges, and Moms for Liberty agitators are not trained lawyers. So, in the hostile confines of besieged school and library boards, legal precedent is often far from anyone's mind. Far more durable of a precedent in this situation is the idea that people tend to feel icky when they hear naughty words, especially in public, and book banners know that. Just as Ralph McIntosh read the most shocking parts of *Howl* to that San Francisco courtroom in 1957, Moms for Liberty and other book banners are reading short but shocking individual passages out loud in school board meetings. They're hoping the shock of hearing naughty words in a non-naughty context will be enough to get school board members and fellow citizens to side with them in their censorious aims. Even if the local politicians are more cautious, or perhaps more aware of actual legal precedent, the shocking passages are often enough to gather support from fellow citizens. For years, the book banners were aided in this by BookLooks. com, which was quite literally a dictionary of the most shocking short passages from a host of book ban usual suspects. After all, what does legal precedent matter to the school board member who's boiling in embarrassment as someone says "fuck" into the microphone? It almost goes without saying that there's massive irony at play here—the book banners are accusing these books of bringing sexual language and content into contexts where it's inappropriate; by reading these passages out loud at school board meetings, the book banners are doing just that.

CHALLENGE WITHOUT READING

I suppose it's maybe too idealistic to hope that everyone trying to restrict access to a book has read the book itself, therefore granting them a nuanced appreciation of the book's appropriateness. It is all too common—perhaps the norm—for book banners to challenge a book without reading it. After all, a salacious passage or two is sufficient to fire up book banning allies, and it's often all the banners need to create a scene at a school board meeting. Sometimes, it's painfully obvious that a banner hasn't read the book in question. In August 2023, Troy, Ohio, resident Bob Eyink challenged nine books in the Troy City School District library. All of them had transgender themes. Eyink found them by looking up the word "transgender" in the school's online library catalog and picking the first nine.[95] He challenged each one of them instantly, without ever holding any of the books in his hand. The ease of filing these challenges, regardless of whether the challenger has read them, can give a parent a tremendous amount of power, allowing huge consequences from an action that could take mere minutes. In July 2024, one Escondido, California, parent challenged one book—*This Book Is Gay* by Juno Dawson. School district officials responded by closing all 23 of the district's libraries to "conduct a thorough audit."[96] One parent, one challenge, one book, thousands of students without vital library access. Remember, the "rights" that the "Parental Rights" movements speak of are only the rights of parents who subscribe to the movement's far-right worldview.

MISUSE WORDS LIKE "PORNOGRAPHY" OR "OBSCENE"

The claim is so common as to be a cliché at this point: school librarians are peddling pornography to vulnerable students. This is a bad faith claim that misunderstands several things, including the job of the school librarian and the very definition of pornography. Still, there they are, Moms for Liberty and their comrades labelling anything with any sexual content at all as pornography, accusing librarians of grooming students and forcing sexuality onto innocent children. It's a shocking argument, and that shock allows the false accusations to spread, but the accusations are just that: false. To explain how absolutely incorrect the pornography claim is, it's worth spending time talking about what pornography actually is and why a YA book with a sex scene absolutely ain't it.

The most common and widely applied legal standard for the definition of pornography is called the Miller Test. In 1971, mail-order pornographer Marvin Miller sent a mass-mailing of a brochure advertising his wares. Somehow a Newport Beach, California, restaurant received five of these brochures. When they arrived, the restaurant owners called the police. Miller was eventually tried and found guilty of violating California Penal Code 311.2(a), a law that prohibits the sale of obscene materials in California. The law was based in part on *Roth v. United States*, the case that helped the judge clear *Howl* since it had some redeeming social value. Miller appealed the verdict all the way to the U.S. Supreme Court on free speech grounds. The Supreme Court agreed to take the case, in part because some of the justices disagreed on the extent to which *Roth* was capable of defining obscene speech. They were eager to revisit the issue, and Miller's case was a perfect chance to do that. Eventually the Supreme Court ruled that the government did have a responsibility to prosecute obscene speech, and that obscene speech was therefore not protected by the First Amendment. But they urged caution in doing so, recognizing the danger of government entities playing fast and loose with the limitation of speech. So they drafted the three-part Miller test, a legal precedent still in place today. It claims that in order for speech to be obscene, you must consider:

1. whether the average person, applying contemporary community standards, would find that the work, taken as a whole, appeals to the prurient interest;

2. whether the work depicts or describes, in an offensive way, sexual conduct or excretory functions, as specifically defined by applicable state law; and

3. whether the work, taken as a whole, lacks serious literary, artistic, political, or scientific value.

All three elements of the test must be true for speech to be prosecuted or limited by the government.

According to some free speech advocates, the Miller Test is controversial and flawed. The idea of "community standards" can easily be abused, for instance, as seen in my own experience teaching high school in Smithville. This vagueness can lead to something being considered obscene in one place and not another, limiting the protection of the artists' free speech rights. But still, despite its flaws, the Miller Test is very clear that a work must be taken as a whole to be determined obscene or not. It is painfully obvious that none of the books that book banners are targeting meet all three points. In fact, you could argue that most of these books don't meet *any* of them. Take Juno Dawson's *This Book Is Gay*, a common book banner punching bag. It's a conversational and educational guide to queerness for young readers. It doesn't shy away from discussing sexual topics, but the Miller Test tells us that the mere presence of sex does not make a book obscene. In terms of step one, perhaps some people might call a young-person's guide to queer sex prurient, but it's important to remember that book banners do not represent the average person, even if they think they do. Book banning remains largely unpopular, and the book ban crisis is driven by a small number of people making a big amount of noise. This minority tends to think they're average people, but in many cases they're extremists who the rest of the community finds kind of annoying. Polling has shown that 62 percent of Americans oppose book bans; even more dramatically, only 1 percent of Americans have engaged in actual book banning attempts. [97] A person who represents just 1 percent of the population can only dubiously claim that they represent the "average." In terms of Miller Test step two, *This Book Is Gay* does describe sexual conduct, but the book is educational, not prurient. Even if that's (somehow) up for debate—there are many on the right that find the mere idea of queer people having sex inherently prurient—number three seals the deal. The book *as a whole* does not lack value. You could argue—and many have, convincingly—that books like *This Book Is Gay* do have value of the literary, artistic, political and/or scientific variety. It's an educational resource utilized and beloved by countless queer teens. I realize these claims could somehow be up for debate, and I'm the kind of person to naturally support a book like *This Book Is Gay*. Still, the thing about the Miller Test is that a book needs to meet *all three criteria*, without any shadow of a doubt. In theory, even a hint of literary merit is enough to clear a book of any obscenity accusations, at least in the court of law.

Knowing this, some book banners are taking on the steep task of renegotiating the Miller Test itself. In 2022, the Utah State legislature enacted HB 374, a bill concerning sensitive materials in schools. Early versions of this bill just plain replaced the Miller Test, claiming it didn't apply in school libraries. Rather than the well-established standard, the original HB 374 defined obscene materials as anything with "gratuitous use of vulgar, profane, or obscene language" or "discussion or representation of sexual conduct." The mere representation of sexual conduct—just a depiction or even discussion of sex—was enough to rule an entire work obscene. The version of the bill that eventually passed thankfully dialed back this language, but the fact that it was even under consideration in the first place is an indication that book banners know the Miller Test is antithetical to their purposes, and they're willing to do something about it. Other branches of government are finding ways to chip away at applying the Miller Test to library books. In 2025, the authors of *And Tango Makes Three* sued Florida's Escambia and Lake County school districts after the book was removed from libraries. The authors claimed the removal was a violation of their free speech. In October 2025, U.S. District Judge Allen Winsor declared that school libraries don't qualify as public forums and, therefore, aren't guarded by free speech protections.[98] If this dangerous idea takes hold, the Miller Test is null and void when applied to school library curation.

A hallmark of the far right and the book ban movement it inspired is a deliberate misuse of language. Censoring gay or BIPOC speech isn't censorship, it's "parents' rights." It's not frank and honest discussion of America's racial history, it's "critical race theory." It's not widespread acceptance of a variety of sexual identities, it's "gender ideology." It's not freedom and acceptance for all, it's "out-of-control wokeness." Of course, it's not books that are honest about the true experiences of young people, sex included, it's "pornography." This is not by accident; it's a deliberate manipulation of language for nefarious needs. To purposefully misconstrue language like this is to take control of the argument and strip it of all nuance. Even if they're flouting decades of legal precedent, as long as they frame the debate in terms of "pornography," they're forcing their opponents to seem like they're defending the right to feed porn to minors. Nobody wants to claim to support that—rightfully so—but this malicious bastardization of language itself allows these book banners to imply that their opponents are all pornographers, even though that's far from the truth. The people more often feeding harmful ideas and language to minors are the book banners themselves.

TAKE OVER SCHOOL AND LIBRARY BOARDS

The book banners are not content just to show up at library board meetings to make noise; many, in fact, are trying to infiltrate school and library boards. Moms for Liberty has a literal handbook for how to launch a successful run for school board, and countless school boards across the country have all of a sudden found themselves composed at least in part of right-wing extremists. This playbook was developed in suburban Texas but has spread nationwide. Mike Hixenbaugh outlines the story well in his excellent book *They Came for the Schools*. Essentially, some racist incidents among students led to a proposed update to the Southlake, Texas, school diversity policy. Then things went absolutely off the rails. A usually routine policy update ignited a political firestorm in Southlake, causing outrage and shouting and false accusations that the schools were indoctrinating students with so-called critical race theory. This inspired several Christian nationalists to run for school board, riding the wave of outrage into municipal government. Of course, connections to wealthy conservative funding networks didn't hurt things, as the campaign became much more visible and mean-spirited than usual.

Once in place, these Christian nationalist radicals began enacting their agenda: ban books, eliminate rights for LGBTQ+ students, and infuse Christianity into the curriculum. Hixenbaugh convincingly argues that all of this is in the service of the ultimate goal for Christian nationalist book banners: the elimination of public schools in America, instead funneling public tax dollars into private religious schools. This won't happen without an influx of fanatics in local, state, and federal education bureaucracies. Book banners are deep into an attempted takeover of the nation's school boards, but it's not inevitable: According to an email from Authors Against Book Bans, November 2025's election day "saw Freedom to Read candidates sweep school board elections in Pennsylvania, Virginia, Texas, Kansas, and everywhere else in the country."

Still, unqualified fanatics are managing their way into influential education posts. There is no more blatantly extreme example of this than the Oklahoma Library Media Advisory Committee. A bit of background: According to *USA Today*, dozens of bomb threats and death threats to hospitals, libraries, and schools—including several Oklahoma institutions—have been documented nationwide in the last two years."[99] There's one commonality linking many if not all of these bomb threats: "In each case, the target of the threats had been targeted in the days before by posts from Libs of TikTok."[100] If you're lucky enough to have never heard of Libs of TikTok, it's a hateful social media channel, with an amazingly huge following, run by a vicious troll named Chaya Raichik. Raichik, in an attempt to "own the libs," regularly uses Libs of TikTok to ridicule (some would say target) LGBTQ+ people. She denies that her posts lead to violence, but the Venn Diagram of places targeted by Libs of TikTok and places that have received bomb threats is basically just a circle. She has refused to denounce these bomb threats. How did Oklahoma officials respond to their state institutions being victim of Raichik's online terror? One official, Oklahoma schools superintendent Ryan Walters, responded by appointing Raichik to the Oklahoma Library Media Advisory Committee. Walters has been called "'the state's top culture warrior' for his opposition to teachers' unions and other conservative targets, including LGBTQ+ students' rights."[101] Raichik and Walters are a match made in hell, and together they've used no less an institution than the State of Oklahoma to go after queer students and the books they read. Chaya Raichik doesn't even live in Oklahoma.

LEGISLATION

It's not just advisory positions and school boards that the book banners are using to bolster their attack. In many cases, they're going straight to the top of state government, trying to pass legislation to formally encode their censoring. Often the basis for this legislation is, once again, the perceived threat of what the far-right radicals falsely call "critical race theory" or "woke ideology." They argue that discussing race is "divisive," which leads to the very strange idea that discussing racism *causes* racism. As the crisis has progressed, the wave of state legislation has become a wave of executive orders from second-term President Trump targeting what he calls "gender ideology," "DEI," and "the woke agenda."

Interestingly, we can trace the critical race theory panic to a single TV appearance. The term was rarely seen in conservative circles until 2020, the year of the uprising after the murder of George Floyd. Notably, this was just months after Nikole Hannah-Jones published the 1619 Project issue of the *New York Times Magazine.* This ambitious project—which argues that an understanding of slavery is fundamental to understanding United States history—made far-right thinkers and politicians apoplectic. Because of Hannah-Jones's ambitious work and the widespread protests against racism, the Trump administration and associated MAGA folks absolutely boiled about any interpretation of American history other than the idea that America is exceptional and good. A right-wing reckoning with race was coming, but rather than protesting or discussing racism itself, they would protest any protest about racism. It all came to a head on September 1, 2020, when far-right activist Christopher Rufo appeared on *Tucker Carlson Tonight* to declare that "critical race theory has pervaded every institution in the federal government," in the process becoming "the default ideology of the federal bureaucracy."[102] Here, it's worth yet another reminder that critical race theory is a very specific legal theory used primarily in law schools. What Rufo was calling CRT is more akin to "being honest about the role race played in American history." Regardless of his obfuscation, which would soon be mirrored by countless Rufo wannabees in library boardrooms across the country, Rufo used his Fox News pulpit to call on President Donald Trump to write an executive order banning CRT from federal agencies. A mere three weeks later, Trump did just that. This is troubling for many reasons, not least of which is legislation by cable news (Rufo surely knew Trump was a regular watcher of Carlson, so he knew exactly what he was doing). Even more troubling is the false framework this flawed notion of CRT gave to far-right legislators and activists. All of a sudden, they had a strawman to respond to. Their response often came in the form of legislation.

In South Carolina, at least eight school districts have anti-CRT policies. The South Carolina legislature has three times passed budgets prohibiting discussion of "divisive concepts" in school (that's a dog whistle if there ever was one). Also in South Carolina,

> In Lexington-Richland School District Five, these educational gag orders resulted in the school board and principal instructing an AP English Language teacher to remove Ta-Nehisi Coates's National Book Award winning memoir *Between the World and Me* from her curriculum in June 2023 because some white students said it made them "ashamed to be Caucasian" and "incredibly uncomfortable." One student claimed that the removals were justified under law, remarking, "I am pretty sure a teacher talking about systemic racism is illegal in South Carolina."[103]

It's not just local or school-level directives, either: of course, Texas's HB 900 is a wildly restrictive book banning bill (more on that later). Florida has the infamous "Don't Say Gay" bill, as well as the Stop WOKE Act (WOKE = Wrongs to Our Kids and Employees), both of which pioneered the banning of so-called CRT and discussion of sensitive topics statewide. In fact, a parallel epidemic to the book banning crisis is the epidemic of educational gag order laws. According to PEN America, "Approximately 1.3 million public school teachers and 100,000 public college and university faculty" are subject to some kind of law or directive that dictates how and what can be discussed in classrooms regarding race or sexual identity, and that number is poised to increase.[104] These laws have very clear aims: "to silence ideas and identities that some find uncomfortable; control narratives about the past; and ensure that only one set of values, viewpoints, and ideologies makes it past the schoolhouse gate."[105] The virus of educational gag orders really is widespread: some kind of legislation restricting classroom discussion of race or LGBTQ+ identities has been passed in New Hampshire, West Virginia, Virginia, North Carolina, South Carolina, Georgia, Alabama, Mississippi, Louisiana, Texas, Oklahoma, Kansas, Arkansas, Missouri, Iowa, Ohio, Indiana, North Dakota, South Dakota, Nebraska, Montana, Idaho, Utah, Arizona, and Alaska.[106] Of course, returning to the subject of this book, these aren't directly book banning bills. But they do lead to book bans: there are many, many documented instances of teachers deciding not to teach a certain book because they're unsure if the book in question runs afoul of their state's anti-CRT legislation.[107] It's all but certain that this soft censorship represents these bills acting exactly as intended. Ultimately, no matter how hard you try, you cannot legislate away discussion of race or sexual identity. But these bills and policies and budgets aren't mere theater, either. They do have at least one major effect: removing books about race and sexual identity from readers who need them.

BULK CHALLENGES

In August 2023, the *Tampa Bay Times* published a thorough analysis of Florida's book ban data for the preceding year. The data found that Florida's book banning activity was surprisingly concentrated. The *Times* reports, "Of the roughly 1,100 complaints recorded in Florida since July 2022, more than 700 came from two counties—Escambia in the western Panhandle and Clay near Jacksonville. Together the two districts make up less than 3 percent of the state's total public-school enrollment."[108] This is a right-wing strategy made macro. Often, as far back as *Howl*, would-be book banners pull an individual passage from a book and make the argument that the whole book is obscene (see #2 on this list). In Florida, book banning activity in two districts is enough to create what author-bookseller Lauren Groff calls an "icy breeze" across the whole state. Again, it doesn't even take a successful challenge to restrict access to a book. Just a climate of puritanism and the threat of punishing teachers can lead to self-censorship.

When it comes to the concentration of Florida's banning activity, even more staggering is the fact that most of it came from two people. According to the *Times*, "About 600 of the complaints came from two people—a Clay County dad and an Escambia County high school teacher."[109] The Clay County dad, Bruce Friedman, has submitted more than four hundred challenges, many of whose complaints are explained only with exclamations like "Protect children!"[110] One of the books he challenged was a picture book featuring PBS's Arthur character because it featured a game of spin the bottle.[111] The Escambia County high school teacher, Vicki Baggett, has filed 178 complaints. Supporters of Bagget's efforts liken children's book *And Tango Makes Three* to putting copies of *Playboy* magazine in school libraries—yet another in the constant parade of examples of right-wing advocates confusing stories about LGBTQ+ people (or penguins) with pornography. Though these complaints make a lot of noise, the issue of barring library access for children isn't popular. One Escambia County school board meeting regular says that Vicki Baggett is "an extreme minority [...] garnering more annoyance than approval among even the county's most traditional-values Republicans."[112] Similarly, Friedman's home district in Clay County allowed parents to opt their children out of library use entirely in 2022, another anti-intellectual feat enabled by Ron DeSantis's legislative crusade (and now echoed nationwide by the Supreme Court's decision in *Mahmoud v. Taylor*). Of the Clay

County School District's 39,000 students, just six were opted out of library use. But while book bans and the tactics of those pushing them aren't necessarily popular, they are effective. When summarizing their report, the *Times* claims, "The data illustrates how a tiny minority of activists across the state can overwhelm school districts while shaping the national conversation over what books belong on school library shelves."[113] And "overwhelm" is the right word: one reason book banners employ this strategy is that a huge number of book challenges drowns librarians in paperwork and bureaucracy. The strategy of creating a torrent of mayhem, a strategy Steve Bannon coined "flood the zone," is a favorite on the far right. The idea of one parent challenging hundreds of books is a small-scale version of the strategy President Trump used while issuing dozens of executive orders in his first two weeks, which together threaten millions of people.

It's important to remember the ultimate goal isn't actually removing books from libraries. The right wing has broader plans, which we'll discuss in the next chapter. All they need to do to advance that agenda is to make noise. And two people in Florida have made a lot of noise filing book challenges. These Florida folks are no anomaly. People are issuing bulk challenges across the country. In Wisconsin's Elkhorn Area School District, "one parent requested that 163 books at Elkhorn Middle School and 281 books at the high school be removed."[114] That's one parent challenging 444 books at once. And in that particular district, books must be removed from shelves while they're being challenged. One parent with radical far-right ideals can wreak a lot of havoc at once. They know this, and they're taking advantage of it. In fact, there's a lot of evidence that this big crisis is largely caused by a small number of people. A *Washington Post* study found that, for the 2021-2022 school year, 60 percent of book bans originated with just 11 parents.[115]

Rely on soft censorship

Of course, a formal challenge leading to withdrawal is just one kind of book ban. We'll call that "hard censorship." An equally successful—if not more successful—strategy to keep books out of the hands of queer or BIPOC readers is to create a climate of fear around the subject of library curation. A rule doesn't need to be enacted to become a rule. A teacher can see another teacher getting harassed. A teacher can hear about threats at a school board meeting. A teacher can see one of their colleagues getting disciplined or fired. A teacher can even see a student promise to have their parents call the school about a certain book. None of these are formal actions; all of them can lead to that teacher making decisions to self-censor their speech or their classroom library. Even if every single formal challenge in the country were unsuccessful, Moms for Liberty and the radical Right have already won the soft censorship battle.

The difficult thing about soft censorship is that it's largely silent. A frightened teacher who decides not to purchase *This Book Is Gay* or *And Tango Makes Three* likely won't call PEN America to self-report their self-censorship. Nonetheless, there is a bit of data to back up the idea that self- or soft censorship is rampant amid Moms for Liberty's climate of fear. One study reports that

> Seven percent of the educators responding have removed books from their classroom or program library due to book bans or challenges; more than twice that indicate they have removed books for other reasons. Regardless of whether educators are experiencing book bans or not, the attention on banned books is affecting the way they teach.[116]

Another study reports, disturbingly, that Black teachers are much more likely to self-censor.[117] It's worth repeating: a book can be banned even if it's not subject to a formal challenging process. A parallel epidemic to the book ban crisis is the crisis of teachers silencing themselves due to a climate of fear.

Soft censorship isn't always an individual choice made by one teacher, either. Another method of soft censorship is to disguise anti-gay curation as "weeding," the normal process of culling books to keep a library current and fresh. Books that are out-dated, old, or beat up get removed from libraries all the time. It's necessary to keep the library up-to-date and responsive to its community. Yet, for example, in Cobb County, Georgia,

> more than 1,600 books were weeded or removed from libraries. The list includes dozens of popular or recently-acquired titles with sex-related content, diverse representation, and many frequently-banned titles. [...] When asked about the district's process behind weeding or removing books, the Superintendent said: 'It has 100 percent to do with the books containing sexually explicit, graphic content.'[118]

Here, a normal process in library maintenance is instead hi-jacked into a de facto bulk ban that requires no due process or community input. Sometimes it goes even further than that: Libraries can just be shut down. Basically, in order to ban some of the books, all of the books are banned. That's exactly what happened in Escondido Union School District in California: One parent challenged *This Book Is Gay*, and the district responded by shutting down all the libraries, as if gay content was like Covid and *This Book Is Gay* was patient zero, waiting to contaminate every other book.[119] In Fort Worth, Texas, the passage of state book-banning bill HB 900 led the school district to shutter every library, asserting that the only way to comply with the law was to thoroughly audit every library title. One hundred books were removed in the process, again without any community input or due process. School districts across the country apply the same thinking to book fairs and author visits: It's better not to do any than risk running afoul of the book banners.

And then there's the ultimate form of soft censorship: quitting your librarian or teacher job. For many professionals working to foster literacy in young people, the climate of fear is just too much. In the wake of Idaho's book banning and anti-CRT legislation, a majority of librarians reported that they were thinking of leaving the profession.[120] Further, a national survey found that nearly a third of superintendents reported teachers leaving their jobs due to stress about school board conflicts.[121] It's clear that Moms for Liberty's climate of fear is harmful to books and the professionals who connect them with kids. It's also bad for the kids. Studies have found that "72 percent of educators indicated that restricting access to certain books decreases students' engagement in reading," and the inverse is also true: access to commonly challenged books *increases* student interest in reading.[122] The damaging effects aren't just pedagogical, either. Pediatrician and co-founder of Authors Against Book Bans, Dr. Sayantani DasGupta, asserts that "being deprived of stories about people like those in your own community is not simply unfair or unjust, it is also deeply unhealthy. Narrative erasure is a kind of psychic violence. Book banning is an assault on our individual and collective health."[123] It's essential to remember that this narrative erasure doesn't only happen through formal bans; the widespread fear and intimidation caused by the banned book crisis is forcing teachers, even those who oppose book bans, to enact it by themselves in their own classrooms.

GO AFTER LIBRARY FUNDING

To some, shutting down a library temporarily for an audit isn't enough. They want the libraries gone permanently. I wrote about one such case in *How to Protect Bookstores and Why*, where the city council in St. Marys, Kansas, tried to shut down their library entirely because one parent challenged *Melissa* by Alex Gino. Only a vast and vociferous community outcry stopped the attempt and kept the library open. St. Marys is far from the only example of a book challenge being turned into an existential attack on the library itself. In her stirring memoir, *That Librarian*, Amanda Jones writes about a backlash against a Drag Story Hour held in a Lafayette County, Louisiana, library. First, a group called Citizens for a New Louisiana started vigorously campaigning against a ballot initiative that would have granted the library system $3.5 million in new millage money. Because of the smear campaign, the initiative failed. Then, the Lafayette City-Parish Council refused to roll forward an older millage, costing the library system an additional $1 million a year. Then, the council voted to take $8 million from the library budget to spend on new sewers instead. All told, these actions cost the library system at least $14.5 million. According to Jones, this led to "the halting of construction projects, loss of staff, fewer materials, and a cutback in programming events for the community."[124] And it didn't even stop there: Two of the leaders of the anti-library campaign were then voted onto the library board.

The shuttering of entire libraries extends to school districts as well. Notoriously, several libraries in Houston Public Schools were converted into discipline centers where reprimanded students watched lessons on computer screens.[125] The move was part of a state takeover of the district, a common occurrence for underperforming school systems. But it's important to remember the context here. A Texas takeover means a takeover by Greg Abbott, a far-right governor who makes no secret of his love of charter schools and the ability to spend public money on private education. This is the guy who signed infamous book-banning bill HB 900, after all. Many parents in Houston fear that "the ultimate goal of state Republican leaders was to undermine support for public education and drive Houston parents to charter or private schools."[126] Many writers and educational thinkers, after all, think the complete dismantling of American public education is the actual, unspoken but central aim of the Moms for Liberty movement. So, it's in this murky context that dozens of Houston school libraries are turned into discipline centers. Shuttering libraries like this is horrifying enough; what's even worse is that these decisions risk creating a racist two-tiered system, where only some schools are losing library access. Houston's mayor says, "You cannot have a situation where you are closing libraries for some schools in certain neighborhoods, and there are other neighborhoods where there are libraries, fully equipped. What the hell are you doing?"[127]

WHEN ALL ELSE FAILS, THERE'S ALWAYS BULLYING

Increasingly, the ire of Moms for Liberty isn't just directed at queer or BIPOC books and readers, but also at library workers themselves. This movement is not above personal attacks and bullying. The bullying is widespread: According to one survey, "About one quarter of principals and one out of ten teachers report being harassed for teaching about race, racism, or bias."[128] To put that number in context, 10 percent of public-school teachers in America equals 380,000 teachers who have been bullied by radical right-wing book banners. Librarians are victims, too: Amanda Jones has been vocal about the harassment she faced after speaking up at a library board meeting in opposition to book bans and censorship. Jones, a school librarian in Louisiana, showed up at a library board meeting after hearing rumors about a board member turning into a book banner, as well as seeing the vague item "Book content and signage" on a meeting agenda.[129] Despite being averse to public speaking, Jones delivered a speech that included sentiments like, "Hate and fear disguised as moral outrage have no place in Livingston Parish."[130] Within days, Citizens for a New Louisiana launched a cyberbullying campaign. Jones was accused of "teaching anal sex to 11-year-olds," "promoting pornography and erotic content to kids," and "grooming an entire generation so that 'they' can feel comfortable and so children will be less resistant to inappropriate advances."[131] Some threatened to show up at her school. One person emailed her to say, "We gunna put ur fat evil PED azz in the dirt."[132] Once a central part of her small community, she felt herself increasingly ostracized, a well-cultivated reputation starting to erode. All this for saying hate and fear don't have a place in that town.

Unfortunately, Jones's experience isn't particularly rare. As previously mentioned, attacks on librarians are coming as public libraries are already stretched thin due to the collapse of the safety net and libraries often being the only indoor places where folks can use the bathroom and generally exist comfortably without being charged for some good or service. This has led to the fact that "librarians have had to act as de facto emergency medical workers or mental health professionals at a moment's notice."[133] Amanda Oliver worked for years at a Washington, D.C., public library in an underserved neighborhood. In her insightful memoir *Overdue: Reckoning with the Public Library*, she writes that libraries are "repositories of language, literature, community care, and human growth. They are also places of objectification, racism, sexual assault, and other human atrocities."[134] The unpredictability, and often unsafety, of library work leads to common and widespread burnout; Oliver went as far as to publish an op-ed called "Working as a Librarian gave me PTSD." One survey of librarians found that "nearly 70 percent of respondents said that they had experienced violent or aggressive behavior from patrons."[135] In her book, Oliver describes a survey she conducted of the librarians she knew, which found that 83 percent of respondents had felt unsafe at work, and nearly three quarters of respondents had experienced empathy fatigue. This climate leaves librarians overextended and burned out. This was all happening before the book ban crisis made things even worse.

On top of the rapid and burnout-inducing expansion of what library work means, now comes the hostility and ruthlessness of the book banners. Not only do librarians have to navigate delicate situations with underserved and mentally ill patrons, but they also have to absorb the attacks from Moms for Liberty and the rest of the hostile movement. People are calling the police on librarians. They're calling them out by name at school board meetings. They're secretly recording conversations with librarians and sharing the videos without consent. They're creating memes about librarians and distributing them in right-wing Facebook groups. It's not just private citizens, either; Virginia state Rep Tim Anderson used FOIA "to learn the identities of librarians at schools that had copies of books some parents complained included sexually explicit material."[136]

Some states are even criminalizing library work, removing traditional protections for library workers and teachers. In Oklahoma, a new law holds librarians and teachers criminally liable for exposing children to obscene content, which is of course a vague sentiment open to malicious interpretation.[137] The culminating effect of this is countless librarians thinking of leaving the profession. As Brooklyn Public Library head librarian Nick Higgins puts it, "People are getting yelled at and screamed at and, after a while, when do you just throw in the towel and say it's not even worth it anymore? And then how do those libraries survive in communities where even the people who are called to that profession don't want anything to do with it anymore because there's so much risk?" Many librarians can't handle the whiplash of going from being perceived as pandemic heroes to grooming, pornographic villains. If the unstated aim of the book ban movement is to dismantle public education and libraries, their ruthless tactics are vicious enough that many formerly devoted librarians are removing themselves from the profession, hastening the decline the far right so desperately wants.

FIGHTING BACK

An understanding of the book banners' strategy is crucial to making a plan for fighting back. Indeed, Moms for Liberty and other book banners are using good strategy for bad aims. The group has a keen sense of the power of community organizing. They have successfully shaped national conversation and policy as a group that started hyper-locally with a few moms. Though they're actually funded by vast amounts of Republican dark money, they retained a local focus by starting similarly small groups in cities and towns nationwide. They also have a deep understanding of the power of local politics. A vast majority of local voters ignore school and library board elections; Moms for Liberty is capitalizing on that apathy to easily snag seats on those very boards. From there, members can shape local politics to their radical agenda. It was these local moves that attracted the attention of the big-name (and big money) national Republican establishment. The idea of starting small and local, community organizing, and capitalizing on local power is just plain good political strategy. Aside from the fact that the Heritage Foundation and the Koch brothers aren't on our side (admittedly, a fairly big obstacle) there's no reason a diverse, pro-book countermovement can't use these local-first strategies to further non-nefarious aims. With that in mind, it's illuminating to take a look at some stories from the library wing of the book ban resistance.

NICK HIGGINS AND BOOKS UNBANNED

One of the direst consequences of the book ban crisis is the lack of access to books. It's important to remember that vulnerable kids are at the heart of this—their access to books that reflect their identity is good for them, and blocking their access to those books is unhealthy. So, a first step in fighting book bans is to restore that access, by whatever means possible. Enter Nick Higgins.

Nick Higgins's office at Brooklyn Public Library's main branch looks lived-in. Piles of books and papers are all over the place, including a dog-eared copy of the vital book *Trouble in Censorville*. Also everywhere are posters for past summer reading initiatives, for instance: a Maurice Sendak illustration and the message, "Go Wild with your Library Card." Leaning against the door is a huge QR code that leads to the website for an initiative called Books Unbanned. I'm here to talk to this busy and energetic man because of this exact program. One of the more prominent institutional responses to date in the book ban crisis, Books Unbanned is a program that allows any teenager in America to sign up for a BPL library card and, therefore, access a digital library of banned books hosted by BPL. Even aside from any legislative or advocacy solutions, Books Unbanned gets right to the heart of the problem: kids' access to books is being threatened, so an important first response is to restore their access. I use the language of first responders on purpose; Higgins frames Books Unbanned in health-emergency terms too, telling me that the program is a "direct intervention with young people across the country who are facing book bans in their local communities. It's almost like an emergency room visit. We get you, you're going through an emergency, here's a library card from an institution out of town, and that'll help you get through."

The idea for Books Unbanned sprouted when one of Higgins's staffers heard about the anti-book activity in Texas, early on, before any of the eventual bills were introduced. Higgins tells me the staffer "came in and she was all excited about it, and she's like, we have to do something. And I'm like, I think you're right. This is really absurd. We started talking and then I was like, well, maybe we can just give everyone in Texas a library card from Brooklyn Public Library." The idea took hold as a way for Higgins and BPL to "bring the fight." But Higgins was hung up on one problem: he didn't want BPL to get a savior complex. He tells me the Texas-only version of the plan "was going to be too much of a spotlight, particularly on libraries that were already in the spotlight for some of this." Ever the dreamer, Higgins's solution to this problem was to open the offer to all kids. Years in, there's plenty of evidence that Books Unbanned working: Higgins tells me that, as of August 2024 when we spoke in Brooklyn, more than 10,000 students have signed up for Brooklyn Library cards. The Books Unbanned website has a repository of testimonials from impacted students. One Utah student says, "Some influential books in my life have since been banned in my school district, and there are still books I have been unable to find access to at my public and school libraries. I am so grateful that I will now have the opportunity to use this card to read freely with more diverse books." Another student, from blue-state Minnesota, says, "They are banning some of my favorite books, and it makes me feel very unwelcome in my school. Thank you for helping me."

The fact that Books Unbanned happened is something of a miracle. Higgins tells me 87 percent of BPL funding comes from local and state funding, so spending that on giving cards to kids in the other 49 states wasn't really an option. For Books Unbanned to work, it would have to be funded by private donations. This presented all kinds of challenges, which were exacerbated by unexpectedly high demand for the program. The initial plan, according to Higgins, was to "run it until the end of the school year, starting in April and ending in June." But then, he adds, "The demand was so intense. We were inundated with emails, social media posts, kids across the country were just clamoring for this kind of support. And so, it created a lot of chaos." The small team—Higgins and two or three others—began to worry about funding. The initial campaign was funded by an anonymous private donor, but they were unable to fund a hugely expanded program ready to meet the high demand. But then an amazing thing happened. According to Higgins, "The more that young people were writing to us and telling their stories and asking for this card, the more people from across the country were writing to us and saying, where can I donate?" As the campaign ramped up, over half of the donations came from outside New York. The support from private donors across the country has easily kept up with demands for electronic banned books from students living in book-ban-happy schools and cities. Books Unbanned went from a quick jolt of inspiration to a nationwide campaign that helped thousands of students access books they'd otherwise be unable to read. Ultimately, Higgins sees Books Unbanned as a positive approach to what is often a very ugly crisis. He says, "The idea behind Books Unbanned was to not get drawn into the fight and talk about the things that they want us to talk about, grooming and all this kind this or that. [Books Unbanned] is really a positive story about why the freedom to read is universal value shared by basically everyone in the country."

CAMERON SAMUELS AND SEAT

It's important to center the idea of getting books into the hands of impacted students, as Books Unbanned is working to do. It's also important to make sure students have a voice in a pro-book response to the banning crisis. One group fighting for just that is Texas's SEAT, or Students Engaged in Advancing Texas. According to their website, SEAT is "a movement of young people developing transferable skills and demonstrating youth visibility in policymaking." Their goal is to involve students in the creation and implementation of policies that impact them; as they write on their website, "Through storytelling and intergenerational partnerships, we're cultivating cultural shifts to center student narratives, promote student rights, and shape a future where students hold agency in education."

SEAT started with a single testimony at a single school board meeting in Katy, Texas, a massive school district with 96,000 students and nine high schools. A very conservative suburb just outside of Houston, Katy also happens to be a hotbed for book banning activity. SEAT founder Cameron Samuels, a former student at Katy ISD, tells me that Katy has long been "at the vanguard of banning books and other forms of censorship and harms against trans people." Now a junior at Brandeis, Cameron still leads the organization, which they say is "working to make sure student voices [are] at the forefront of these conversations about books and curriculum and libraries and what was acceptable for us to teach in schools." Cameron's work has drawn national attention and achieved some real change in Texas and beyond, but the whole endeavor had humble beginnings. Cameron tells me that an inflection point for their activism was being a sixth grader watching the ramp-up to the 2016 election. Some of it went over their head but they understood enough to be concerned; after all, they tell me, "Children know a lot more than what adults think." They knew enough to realize that their "being LGBTQ, being Jewish, being disabled—these sorts of things were just not compatible with Trumpism." From a morass of violence and political hatred came Cameron's determination to claim that seat at the table. There's a lot of evidence that they have accomplished this.

During Cameron's junior year, Katy ISD suddenly cancelled an October 4, 2021, author event by Jerry Craft, author of award-winning graphic novels *Class Act* and *The New Kid*. The Katy ISD superintendent said the cancellation was due to "one formal challenge" of Craft's books.[138] The lone challenge accused Craft's work of promoting critical race theory, which of course actually means what Christopher Rufo *considers* critical race theory. The challenge and cancellation occurred a month after Texas passed a "divisive concepts" "anti-CRT" bill, surely influencing Katy ISD's decision. Because of the cancellation of Craft's talk, Cameron signed up to speak at the next Katy ISD school board meeting.

Cameron Samuels is an unlikely candidate for stepping up to speak at a hostile school board meeting; they tell me, "I wasn't ever necessarily the spokesperson or the confident person in front." But something about the political moment stirred something in Cameron that led them to that microphone. It certainly seems like the catalyst for Cameron to speak up was the absolute lack of student voices in the debate up to that point; they tell me, "We're experts of our lived experience and we want to create impact." And so, Cameron found themself at the microphone, terrified, speaking up about the ham-fisted book banning in Katy as well as other issues like a homophobic internet filter on school computers. A quick glance at the minutes from the November 15, 2021, Katy ISD board meeting reveals what Cameron was up against. Even the person taking the minutes has absorbed the book ban movement's misappropriation of words like "pornography." This is the entirety of the public comment section of the meeting:

- Mary Ellen Cuzela spoke regarding library audits, obscene books and critical race theory.
- Luis Salinas spoke regarding discrimination against children with disabilities.
- Victor Perez spoke regarding books in Katy ISD libraries.
- Cameron Samuels spoke regarding technology filters on campus.
- Donna McElmurry spoke regarding obscene library book.
- Jennifer Adler spoke regarding books in public schools.
- Anita Nelson spoke regarding pornography in school libraries.
- Karen Perez spoke regarding inappropriate books in Katy ISD libraries.
- Claudia Turcott spoke regarding reading materials available in Katy ISD and critical race theory.

Indeed, Cameron's testimony was not welcomed by the crowd in the room. Cameron is quoted saying, "I was the only student in the room. There was no applause. I felt isolated and lonely, but I had to keep fighting for this because I had peers who were directly affected by these policies"[139] In another telling of the story, Cameron showed a politics-ready flair for the soundbite when they told *NBC News*, "That was really frightening as I walked back to my seat after speaking and just saw people staring at me, but I realized that those stares were stairs to climb on."[140] Regardless of the chilly reception (or perhaps because of it), Cameron grew determined to return, and bring allies with them to the next meeting. They tell me, "One month after that first time, in December, we returned to the school board meeting and we had more people; we wanted to pack the board meeting, so we got more people there." Then they went to the January meeting. February too. All told, Cameron spoke at five consecutive Katy ISD school board meetings, bringing more students with them each time, making sure at bare minimum that student voices were part of the discussion. They had some success: They gathered thousands of signatures for a community petition. They got some sites unblocked from the web filter. But the book ban fight was losing ground: Cameron tells me, "More books were being pulled off of shelves." In early 2022, it became clear to Cameron and company that more direct action was necessary to get banned books into the hands of readers who needed them. So they got to work.

Cameron's focus on books is no accident; they are clearly a lifelong reader. They tell me that "growing up, there weren't often books that really affirmed or gave words to my LGBTQ identity. I've known I've been different, but I never had the words to describe it." So, testimony at school board meetings was never going to be enough for Cameron and their friends. They needed to get banned books into the hands of students, especially closeted students or students who came from families that were unsupportive of their queer identities. So they reached out to publishers. Books began arriving by the dozen, by the hundred. Cameron says, "Boxes and boxes of books continued being delivered. We didn't know how many were going to be delivered, but they just kept coming on in." It would be no easy task to distribute hundreds of books that a significant portion of the Katy community called pornography. It would require strategy. It would likely require the complete circumvention of any grown-ups at all. They'd need a student-to-student underground distribution network, and that's precisely what they built.

As the organization that was slowly becoming SEAT considered how exactly to distribute hundreds of books in a city with a strong anti-book current, they realized that they already had the key. They were a student-led organization building a network of likeminded folks. All they had to do was reach out to other student-led organizations. In January 2022, Cameron and their comrades took to social media to find people at Katy's nine high schools whose student clubs might help distribute banned books. "We realized that clubs already have an audience, they have a network of people," Cameron tells me. Word spread, interest grew, and clubs across Katy got in touch. Once everyone was made aware of policies and local regulations, it was time to prepare the actual books for distribution. Taking advantage of a day off school, the newly assembled network gathered in a Katy park to slip fliers into the books and pack them for distribution to individual schools. The public nature of this in a place like Katy was risky, but the students were unfazed. In fact, the gathering was even joyful. Cameron reminisces about their parents bringing their dog by on a walk. The whole gathering was permeated by a sense of solidarity. Cameron calls it "a community of like, 'we're going to do this.' We got the enthusiasm. We're here for each other. No matter what happens in the next week, we are doing it. We're in the midst of it." And instead of withering under possible public pressure, the students were ready for the spotlight: they had reviewed talking points, and good thing, since several journalists showed up to do news reports and individual interviews. In the week that followed, the ad hoc underground student-led book distribution network passed out more than two hundred books, with hundreds more to follow later that spring.

Listening to Cameron tell me about these efforts, I can't help but be impressed by the smart organizing they showed with their SEAT team. Rather than build from the ground up, they activated existing networks. They built partnerships with other organizations. They wrote and shared talking points. They ensured media coverage at prominent public events. These kids are 16, 17, 18 years old in a town that's hostile to their identities and their reading habits, but here they are demonstrating skillful political organizing. When I ask Cameron how the heck they knew how to do all this, they explain that much of their strategy came from being surrounded by journalists as a child. "I had that kind of journalistic lens because my family has a line of journalists all the way back to my great-grandmother and great-grandfather and so on. I wasn't a professional journalist, but I guess I was seeing things from the perspective of a journalist," they tell me. In addition to shaping Cameron's view on how to frame a story for the press, their parents are also supportive of their efforts. "I was very fortunate to have supportive parents, and so I had a great community back home," they tell me. Of course, the irony is that parents like Cameron's, parents who fight for their queer kids and their right to read whatever they want, apparently don't qualify for the "rights" the so-called "parents' rights" movement is pushing for.

Another irony is that this movement that claims to be so hell-bent on protecting kids can be actively hostile to kids that are outside that worldview. How can anyone credibly claim to be protecting kids when they're publicly attacking them? Despite their supportive family, Cameron has nonetheless felt the wrath of adults in the Katy community. They tell me that they were subject to all kinds of abuse:

> School board candidates doxxing me and other students in this with some negativity and threats, intimidation at the schools that we distributed banned books at, those in the community repeatedly calling the district saying that we're distributing what they thought was pornography and they needed to arrest us, or they needed to shut down our efforts and to have the security heightened at schools across the district for them to not allow any visitors and

lock the doors after school to escort me home. No 17-year-old should have been put through any of that.

But none of it deterred Cameron, who continued their efforts through it all.

Another thing that no 17-year-old should have been put through was a lie-filled, hostile grilling by one of the most radical right-wing U.S. Senators. But that's exactly what happened on September 12, 2023, at a Senate Judiciary Committee hearing when Senator John Kennedy publicly confronted Cameron, who had traveled to Washington to testify in a hearing about book bans called by Illinois Senator Dick Durbin. When Senator Kennedy began his turn, he opted for the tried and true "quote out of context" strategy:

> Let's take two books that have been much discussed. The first one is called *All Boys Aren't Blue*. I will quote from it. "I put some lube on and got him on his knees. I began to slide into him from behind. I pulled out of him and kissed him. He asked me to turn over while he slipped a condom on himself. This was my ass, and I was struggling to imagine someone inside me. He got on top and slowly inserted himself into me. It was the worst pain I think I have ever felt in my life. Eventually I felt a mix of pleasure with the pain." *All Boys Aren't Blue*. The second is another much-discussed book. I'm sure you are familiar with it. It is called *Gender Queer*. Let me read an excerpt from that. "I got a new strap-on harness today. I can't wait to put it on you. It will fit my favorite dildo perfectly. You're going to look so hot. I can't wait to have your cock in my mouth. I'm going to give you the blowjob of your life, then I want you inside of me."

When Kennedy tried to pivot his questioning to Cameron, the senator stumbled through a bunch of clumsy misgendering, unable to think of an honorific other than "Mr." or "Ms.," eventually settling upon just "Cameron." Cameron responded with a simple, "It's pronounced Mx." Throughout Kennedy's hostile questioning, Cameron managed to land some good lines: "Senator, your definition of sexual is synonymous with LGBTQ identity." "*GenderQueer* has never been in my school library, so it's never been banned." "That scene in *All Boys Aren't Blue* is about sexual abuse, it's not erotic." Cameron kept a level head and a straight face the entire time. Their performance was enough to capture the attention of Cameron's favorite childhood author, Rick Riordan, who tweeted in support of them. Cameron tells me, "Reading [Riordan's Percy Jackson] series, the way that it's a limitless and mythical world [...] I feel like Rick Riordan's writing was really incredible. So, to see that he and his wife had watched my Senate testimony to Congress? It was really remarkable to look on Twitter and see that they posted about it." It's important to remember that there are just as many Rick Riordans as there are Senator John Kennedys. It's also important to know that, remarkable as they are, I have to imagine there are more Cameron Samuelses out there.

Undeterred as ever, Cameron's eye is on the future. They're still heavily involved from Brandeis, helping to lead the movement they created. 2025 brings a new legislative session in Texas, with book ban crusaders promising even more mayhem and censorship. Pre-filed bills for the 2025 session include several expanding state funding for private schools, one that removes local control over school library materials, *ten* that would work towards criminalizing library work, and one that promises to eliminate the Miller Test to redefine "harmful materials" in a way that makes it much easier to arrest booksellers for selling "divisive" books.[141] One book banning law has already been implemented: SB 13, which transfers school library curation duties from librarians to school boards. It also stipulates that parental advisory councils can take over that duty from school boards if as few as 50 parents in a community sign a petition to establish a council. But it's not all bad news, and there's some proof that opposition to these laws might work: SB 3225, which would have placed severe limitations on libraries' right to allow access to "sexually explicit" books (with a broad and imprecise definition of such) died in the chamber without a final vote.

Is Cameron ready to keep fighting? Of course. "The first rule of democracy is not to surrender your power to those in authority when they ask for it," they say, adding,

> We want to have a big part in the legislative session and centering student narratives. We have a variety of issues that we're focused on where we can be the authors of our stories and the history that we're living in. It's all going to continue ramping up. Christian nationalism, defunding public education, harming LGBTQ students and banning books . . . all of these issues intersect. It's about what's acceptable in our current societal norms and who gets a voice, who matters. So we're trying to hold the line. We're trying to speak above the flood line of censorship, and we have a lot of work to do.

It's frankly impressive to hear Cameron discuss this, how mature their interview-ready voice and rhetoric are. It doesn't feel like talking to a college student at all; they're wise beyond their years. I imagine part of the reason for that is just what they've gone through in the past few years, not only advocating tirelessly but also weathering abuse from the adults who at least profess to protecting children. "It should not have been my responsibility as a 17-year-old to lead this movement," they tell me, continuing, "With censorship being a means to suppress people, it's never been about the books, it's never about the appropriateness of content. It's about the ideas and the identities that these books and stories represent the voices and people behind them."

👉 HOW TO DEFEND BOOKS

DO NOT COMPLY IN ADVANCE

Early in the second Trump administration, a simple dictum from Timothy Snyder's *On Tyranny* circulated on social media: "Do not comply in advance." Just because the book banners are loud and determined doesn't mean we need to give up without a fight. Nick Higgins didn't let hostile school districts prevent all access to banned books for teens nationwide. Cameron Samuels didn't let a chilly, if not hostile, reaction at his first school board testimony stop them. Rather, they just brought more students with them next time. Just because a violent minority of people are trying to ban books, doesn't mean you need to play their game. Stick to your guns, because a large majority of people (not to mention courts) are on our side. If you're a teacher or librarian, you can resist the pull of soft censorship, relying on library policies and legal precedent to guide your book decisions instead of noise from the vocal minority of book banners. If you're a parent, be deliberate about providing a wide range of perspectives in the books your children read. If you're a reader, pursue and support stories from all backgrounds, especially those who have been victim to state violence.

UNDERSTAND BOOK BANNERS' STRATEGY

To defeat an enemy requires a detailed knowledge of their strategy. If we go into a school board meeting prepared for passages to be read out of context and mislabeled as "pornography," we won't be subject to the shock value of book banners' tactics, and thus we'll be able to keep a clear head to make rational arguments. This requires preparation: Know what relevant policies, laws, and legal precedents actually say, rather than what book banners want you to think they say. Book banners may win the war of vibes in a school board meeting, but they rarely win in court. They do their homework, make sure you do yours. If you're well-armed with strong arguments, you have a better chance of being a voice of reason that cuts through book banners' hysterical noise.

Another way to co-opt book banners' strategy is to organize. Even though they're not-so-secretly funded by Republican establishment dark money, Moms for Liberty is still pretty good at community organizing. It started locally and successfully brought its concerns into a national spotlight. We can do that, too. Just look at Cameron Samuels, who started by connecting student organizations to distribute banned books student-to-student across Katy, Texas, and eventually ended up testifying before a U.S. Senate committee. The book ban movement has again and again proved that a small number of passionate parents can cause a lot of mayhem; they do not have a monopoly on this fact, so find some folks who agree with you and make some mayhem to protect the right to read.

ENSURE ACCESS TO BOOKS

Do not forget that the harm of all this doesn't fall on squabbling adults; it falls on vulnerable students who are losing access to books that can sometimes be literally lifesaving. As you fight back, remember to center student voices and ensure that they can access these books even if hostile adults in their communities don't want them to. Look for stories like Cameron Samuels's, and know about resources like Books Unbanned. Support book access projects financially with donations of money or books. Coordinate with likeminded teachers to help them preserve access to vital books. Check in with the librarians in your community about what they need. In fact, the librarians are probably already telling you. In spring 2025, the Ohio state budget contained a provision that would drastically and lastingly cut library funding in the state. In the wake of the budget's release, I got an email from every library system I've ever used, each one calmly and clearly explaining how to contact my reps and even what to say to resist this budget provision. Ultimately, due to a rapid and extensive wave of public opposition, Governor Mike DeWine line-item vetoed the library funding shift.

SHOW UP

It'd be hard to argue that Cameron Samuels hasn't made a difference in Katy, Texas, and even nationwide. Their first step in that journey was the short walk from the seats in the school board meeting room to the microphone. They are an embodiment of one of the most important ways to defend books: show up. The book banners are so good at showing up. They're at every school and library board meeting, they're on every social media network, they even show up to librarians' houses (please don't do this). Showing up saved a library in St. Marys, Kansas. Showing up got the Katy, Texas, school internet filter to stop blocking sites like the Trevor Project. Showing up can demonstrate the reality that most people don't actually support book bans. Don't let the 1 percent of people who are book banners take up 100 percent of the space in the room.

CHAPTER 3: BOOKSTORES AS BEACONS OF TOLERANCE

O n a desperately humid New Orleans morning in summer 2024, about 30 booksellers have gathered in a second-floor conference room at the Sheraton on Canal Street. It is the first day of the American Booksellers Association's annual Children's Institute, and this early-rising group of booksellers are huddled in small groups, planning Drag Story Hour events. Spread before them on the table are descriptions of hypothetical bookstores, the towns they are in, and floor plans and blueprints of the stores themselves. A tiny bookstore/café in a tourist town. A bustling downtown shop. A small store in a rural area. Every time the groups near a final vision for their story hour events, a complication arises. Someone has written an angry op-ed in the local paper, denouncing Drag Story Hours as "grooming" events. A Facebook post about the event has gone viral in the wrong way, attracting a lot of far-right attention. The police have received a tip that Proud Boys are planning on demonstrating at the event. The drag queen herself has accused the local private security firm of racism. As each complication arises, each group must decide how to proceed with their event, or if they should even try to have it in the first place.

The session we are attending, "Event Safety by Drag Story Hour," is less presentation than tactical strategy session. Though these bookstore events are hypothetical, they are completely based in reality. Countless bookstores and other venues have grappled with these decisions and obstacles for years. It is a sad reality that hosting a Drag Story Hour—a fun, cheerful, all-ages event designed to hook children on reading and provide a safe space for all kids—now requires a detailed safety plan. By request, I'm not including details of the new framework DSH has developed for hosting their events, but suffice to say it requires weeks or even months of planning, careful strategizing, and a flotilla of volunteers. Hearing Jonathan and Regan from DSH talk about safely planning an event involves language usually employed for protests or political actions. That's no mistake—DSH's new safety framework stems from years of working alongside activists and organizers with similar goals of protecting and providing space for LGBTQ+ folks. In recent years, it's become clear that such work requires more ingenuity and planning.

There's always been some opposition to Drag Story Hours since their founding in 2020, but according to DSH Executive Director Jonathan Hamlit, around 2022 things got really intense. He tells me, "After *Roe v. Wade* [was repealed] and after the [January 6th] insurrection, things just really ramped up and gave people permission to get more violent and more organized with opposition. I think that's where we saw a big change with this increased rhetoric of transphobia and homophobia and hating drag." The need for an organized safety plan became obvious when a June 2022 story hour in San Lorenzo, California, was attacked by a group of Proud Boys. According to Hamlit, "Before then it was just like your Westboro Baptist style kind of protest. [The San Lorenzo event] was very different and it was really scary. They came with AK-47 T-shirts and were flashing their white supremacy hand signals and things like that." Public safety is not really what brought Hamlit to Drag Story Hours in the first place: "I never wanted to be part of a movement. I never wanted to be an activist. I'm a drag queen that loves working with kids, so this way I can do a day gig and then also night life at the same time. And then here I am eight, nine years later doing active shooter Stop the Bleed safety trainings at conferences around the country." So how did Hamlit go from a Drag performer looking for daytime gigs to a political organizer teaching booksellers community safety? How did hosting a Drag Story Hour become an endeavor that requires tactical strategy and coordination of an army of employees? And what can people—readers, booksellers, policymakers, citizens—do about it? As much as Drag Story Hour's antagonists try to hide behind a smokescreen of caring about children, attacks on events like Drag Story Hour are attacks on readers and the books they love. But, as demonstrated by the creative and unceasing organizers of Drag Story Hour, there is much to be done to defend them.

ATTACKS ON DRAG STORY HOURS

Tara Lipsyncki and Mosaics

Drag queen Tara Lipsyncki came to drag after a career as a professional ice skater, most recently as Goofy and other NDA-protected characters for Disney on Ice. "I was Buzz Lightyear's friend," she tells me. A dedication to performing and a passion for children's entertainment led Lipsyncki to drag. She established some regular shows at venues in and around her hometown of Provo, Utah. Then, in August 2022, one of the shows, Spill the Tea, was targeted by Chaya Raichik's aggressive far-right social media account Libs of TikTok. Lipsyncki became the target of overwhelming online hate, and the tea shop that hosted the show withered a barrage of negative reviews online. The harassment reached a fever pitch in January 2023, when a group of Proud Boys toting AR-15s showed up outside of Spill the Tea.

"From that moment on, it became clear that this was going to get worse before it got better," Lipsyncki tells me, and she's right. First of all, a moral panic erupted in the city councils of Utah: Lipsyncki says, "I was the subject of so many city council meetings in Vernal, Utah; St. George, Utah; Logan, Utah; Rock Springs, Wyoming; all of it. And they're like, 'Tara's a groomer, Tara's a pedophile.'" A new nadir of the harassment came in September 2023, when Lypsyncki was slated to host a Drag Story Hour at Salt Lake City bookstore landmark the King's English. Lipsyncki started hosting Drag Story Hours at the King's English in June 2023, and for a few months there were no issues. But then in September, as Lipsyncki was unlocking her car to drive to that month's event, King's English owner Calvin Crosby called her to tell her that the store had received a bomb threat. The event was cancelled, and the store was closed for the day. The far right had once again interrupted children's access to diverse, joyful literary programming. I wish I could say that's the only threat Lipsyncki has received for her work in Utah. A few months later, in December 2023, the online group Gays Against Groomers doxxed Lipsyncki and her husband, posting their legal names, home address, phone numbers, and more online. Lipsyncki tells me, "They wanted people to find me and kill me. So, I had to sell my childhood home and go into hiding." Lipsyncki had recently sold her house and moved into her childhood home; the people who bought her previous home were swatted. In the midst of all this, it became clear to Lipsyncki that something needed to be done. Even though nobody could blame her for lying low and disappearing for a while, she instead sprang into action.

"It became clearer and clearer to my husband and me that what is needed is a physical safe space that is accessible to all ages," Lipsyncki tells me. That safe space eventually became Mosaics, a hybrid bookstore, community center, and event space. Lipsyncki tells me, "I felt the need to create a safe space for college kids, high school kids, and middle school kids to have a safe affirming space. Utah County has the highest suicide rate in the state of Utah and the third highest in the nation, especially with LGBTQ youth." Lipsyncki explains that "a lot of queer people don't make it out of here alive, just because of the social pressure to be perfect, be Mormon, have a wife, have kids, whatever." It's for this reason that Mosaics is primarily "a 501(c)(3) that does housing and health and education services," and the used books help to pay for the education and advocacy work. Of course, Mosaics hosts Drag Story Hours—12 of them, to be precise. They've received bomb threats for those, too. The risk of hosting Drag Story Hour even shaped the architecture of the store. Lipsyncki shows me the layout, including the sealed-off event space with a secure, unmarked door visible from the cash register. In the back of the event space, she shows me the emergency second exit that leads to the back room and its garage door. That garage door has an emergency switch so it can open quickly in case people need to flee. I've never seen a bookstore designed with such emergency preparedness in mind. So why face all this hate? Why doesn't Lipsyncki just move somewhere else to start over? When I ask her this, she answers defiantly:

> People tell us, you can't do that. I say, "Hold my beer," and I'm going to do it, and I'm going to prove you wrong. What are these powers that are trying to silence me actually going to do? They've already taken my home, they've bankrupted me, they've taken my health, they've taken my safety. What are you going to do now? Really at the end of the day? I have nothing to lose by just being loud and taking the resources from those that don't need them and giving them to those who do.

Even though Utah County, Utah, is a hostile place for such work, Tara Lipsyncki remains dedicated to Drag Story Hour specifically and providing safe community environments for queer youth in general. But it's not easy or self-sustaining work. In Fall 2024, Mosaics launched Save Mosaics, a $200,000 Indiegogo campaign claiming, "Without help, Mosaics will be forced to close its doors by December 1, 2024." The campaign raised $70,000, enough to keep Mosaics open, at least for a little while. In late August 2025, Mosaics finally announced that they were closing their physical location permanently, with plans to transition to a mobile model. They're going to move event programming into community spaces across the Mountain West, despite the risks. In a statement on Instagram, Mosaics wrote, "we will continue to fight for those the system leaves behind [...] that fight is far from over."

BUFFALO STREET BOOKS

Don't think for a moment that this kind of thing only happens in places like Utah or Texas or Florida or Iowa or Arkansas. In *The ABA Right to Read Handbook*, Philomena Polefrone writes, "There's a misconception among many in so-called 'blue states' that book bans are something that happen somewhere else. That misconception has allowed book bans to spread around the country."[142] Just ask the staff and board members of Buffalo Street Books, a nonprofit bookstore in Ithaca, New York. Ithaca is a terrifically charming college town tucked into the mountains of central New York. It has one of the best Farmers' Markets I've ever seen, located on a picturesque riverbank in a sprawling, weathered wood pavilion. The downtown is a pedestrian-friendly joy to wander, with a four-block car-free mall marching its way through a charming collection of small businesses. Locals love to tell you about their favorite hikes to one of several waterfalls in the surrounding area. There are three bookstores downtown. One of them, Buffalo Street Books, has been hosting Drag Story Hours since 2018. Lisa Swayze, general manager of Buffalo Street Books, tells me the whole idea behind the Drag Story Hour events was to bring joy into the bookstore: "We really wanted to take advantage of the *fun* of Drag Story Hour." Hosting these jubilant events in such a welcoming, liberal city meant Buffalo Street had no problems or backlash. Until April 7, 2024, that is.

The first that Lisa Swayze heard of it was a Buffalo Street Books board member calling to tell her that the police were at her house, scanning the perimeter for any explosives. They did the same at the houses of a few other board members. They even tried to do so at the home of a 22-year-old part-time bookseller, but she had moved away from the childhood home listed on her driver's license. Of course, that meant that her parents had the lovely surprise of opening the door to the police telling them there was a bomb threat against their daughter's workplace. Finally, the police called the store to tell them that a bomb threat had been issued against it. At first, the police were not forthcoming with information. Swayze tells me, "We just had a ton of questions for them at that point, which they wouldn't answer right away." The news, and the vagueness surrounding it, sent a chill through the bookstore and its workers. "All this stuff that we didn't know right away that made it actually scarier than when we really found out what happened," Swayze tells me. She adds, "We were frightened. It's scary." Questions abounded: what, if anything, do we tell our community? Should we continue with the Drag Story Hours? Who are these people who are threatening us? And what did they say?

Eventually, the police shared more information with the Buffalo Street team. Turns out, the threat had been emailed to a TV news station in Buffalo, an apparent misreading of the name of the store. The Buffalo station forwarded the threat to a news station in Syracuse, which sent it along to the Tompkins County Sheriff. Though the person writing the threat didn't research the store's location particularly well, they did do enough due diligence to name a few board members and a bookseller in the threat. And it was all pretty violent, which made it unnerving: Swayze tells me, "Literally the language was, 'we are going to kill you.' So that didn't make anybody happy to hear that." Eventually, the police did share the threat with Buffalo Street, who shared it with me. It came with the subject line, "We placed a bomb in various locations in the Dewitt Mall," the building that houses Buffalo Street and other small businesses. The text of the email reads:

> Today at around 12:15 our bombs will blow up the Dewitt Mall at 215 N. Cayuga Street. You are disgusting degenerates, pedophiles, groomers, child abusers. You are promoting degeracy [sic] and preying upon our children and we are not going to stand idly by as you enact your sick fetishes fuck with our children's minds. We will fucking kill you.

> This is our hit list; these people have already been assassinated, or they soon will be we placed bombs in their homes, we will blow up their houses and kill them and their families. We will shoot anyone who survives.

The email continues to list five names, presumably Buffalo Street board members and booksellers, as well as their home addresses. The email threatened that the bombs would go off at 12:15 on April 7; at that time, Buffalo Street Books would be in the middle of a Drag Story Hour.

In large part because of the Buffalo confusion, the police determined that the bomb threat wasn't credible. Also, it seems that identical threats had appeared across the country; a Lieutenant for the Tompkins County Sheriff emailed the store to say that he "did hear back from the FBI yesterday and after a couple days to gather information they did determine that the language in the email threat was seen multiple times at different locations throughout the county over the weekend." Still, Buffalo Street Books had to figure out what to do and who to tell. They decided on being transparent with their community. A factor in this decision was the fact that, at the time of the threat, Buffalo Street was operating as a consumer-owned coop. Swayze explains, "We're so connected to the community here. It felt like they should know [about the bomb threat]. After all, half of them are owners of the store!" Thinking about how to recover was also part of their decision to share the news: "We wanted people to know because we wanted to feel supported," Swayze says. On April 9, two days after the threat, the board sent a cake to the booksellers, and Swayze posted a picture of it on Instagram with a promise for more information about the bomb threat soon. More info came a few days later, on April 12, when Swayze issued a full statement via email to the Buffalo Street mailing list. It read, in part:

> If anything, the threat only increases our resolve to continue to do the things that we believe improve lives and spread love through books in our community. In particular, Drag Story Hour does all of those things beautifully. We are grateful to our Drag Queens who volunteer their time to spread literacy and joy so kids can be confident in themselves and changemakers in their communities. We remain committed to inclusion and equity and to the bookstore being a safe community space for all.

Due to their role as a community anchor and their unwavering dedication to inclusive programming, the store received a wave of support. But I hesitate to call this a happy ending—for one thing, the ideal version of this story doesn't feature a bomb threat at all. Nobody deserves to be threatened, especially if the threat is inspired by inclusive and joyful programming for children. And second, despite the post-threat support, Buffalo Street Books is encountering tough times like so many other bookstores in 2024. They're hoping a switch to a nonprofit model will help them access enough funding to overcome their consistent budget short-falls. But it is still uncertain, and the uncertainty is made worse by the possibility of being threatened for doing such important work. But one thing is clear: Even liberal cities are under threat from the right wing's assault on the right to read. Swayze says,

"Don't take it for granted that you're safe because you're in a more liberal community, I don't think any of us are safe from any of this." This is, of course, true. But also true is the idea that much of the inspiration for this everywhere attack comes from Texas.

BOOK BANNING VIA LEGISLATION
THE READER ACT

You'd think a bill that promises to ban beloved Texas classic *Lonesome Dove* would have a hard time passing the Texas statehouse. Yet that's exactly what Frisco, Texas, representative Jared Patterson promised in a hearing about the bill he authored, HB 900, also known (with apparently no intended irony) as the READER Act. In that March 2023 hearing of the House Public Education Committee, Round Rock Democrat James Talarico tried to catch Patterson in a trap: Because *Lonesome Dove* contains depictions of sex, would it too be banned from classrooms like so many other books under the READER Act? Patterson fell right into the trap. After admitting he hadn't read the book, he said that if the book indeed contained the lurid passages Talarico was alluding to, well then, "they might need to ban *Lonesome Dove.*"[143] Despite the potential blunder of threatening to ban the unofficial Texas State Book, Patterson was ultimately successful in passing HB 900, one of the strictest book ban bills ever passed, not to mention one that Patterson admits can serve as "model legislation for the rest of the nation."

Jared Patterson was born in 1983. It is unclear if he is much of a reader. I wanted to ask him about it, but he and his office ignored several requests for interviews. What is clear is that Patterson is the most conservative member of the Texas legislature, which is quite a feat. Apparently, Patterson's interest in how libraries are curated began in 2021 with the help of another super-conservative Texas rep, Matt Krause. On October 25, 2021, Krause, in his capacity as chair of the dystopian-sounding Texas House Committee on General Investigating, sent a letter to several school superintendents statewide (at the time, Krause refused to disclose exactly who got the letter). Attached to the letter was a list of 850 books. In his letter, Krause demanded that each superintendent find the books in their district and list how much was paid for them, as well as identifying any other books in their district that "address or contain the following topics: human sexuality, sexually transmitted diseases, or human immunodeficiency virus (HIV) or acquired immune deficiency syndrome (AIDS), sexually explicit images, graphic presentations of sexual behavior that is in violation of the law, or contain material that might make students feel discomfort, guilt, anguish, or any other form of psychological distress because of their race or sex or convey that a student, by virtue of their race or sex, is inherently racist, sexist, or oppressive, whether consciously or unconsciously."

Of course, much of this is absurd. Superintendents had until November 12 to answer—18 days. But the biggest absurdity was the list itself. Krause did not share his methodology in drafting it, perhaps because there wasn't one. It's most likely a list of books that just had offensive vibes in the mind of Krause and his team. The list of course had book-ban usual suspects like *Gender Queer* and *Lawn Boy*. But it also included books that were banal (*Inventions and Inventors* by Roger Smith), actually educational (*Avoiding Bullies? Skills to Outsmart and Stop Them* by Louise Spilsbury), and downright ironic (*The Year They Burned the Books* by Nancy Garden).[144] Sloppy methodology, inexplicable political bullying, headline-grabbing posturing: It is of note that, at the time he sent his list, Krause was running in a crowded field for Texas Attorney General. In all likelihood, queer kids and the books they read were just an easy way for Krause to score political points. Attempts to ban books are almost never out of actual concern for children.

Despite the fact that Krause's list was a craven political stunt, it inspired one ambitious Texas lawmaker to take action. In August 2022, less than a year after Krause issued his demands, Jared Patterson issued formal challenges to about 28 books in his hometown school district, Frisco ISD. But Patterson was not satisfied keeping his fight in his home district alone; when a Texas legislative session began in January 2023, Patterson was ready to take his crusade statewide. Patterson authored and introduced HB 900, which he called the READER Act (READER = "Restricting Explicit and Adult Designated Educational Resources"). The provisions of the bill stipulate that any vendor selling books to public schools in Texas would have to rate each book for sexual content. Required ratings include "sexually explicit" and "sexually relevant." Sexually explicit materials currently in use must be recalled and never sold to schools again. Sexually relevant materials can only be accessed with parent permission. Vendors are required to impose these ratings not only on future books sold to schools or libraries, but on all past books sold that are still in use. The vendors supply the ratings, but the Texas Education Association reserves the right to deem ratings incorrect. If TEA issues a correction that a vendor refuses to implement, the vendor is forever prohibited from selling books to schools in Texas. Allow me to speak as a former bookseller here: It is not controversial to say that these conditions are impossible. Under HB 900, bookstores across Texas would be essentially unable to sell books to schools at all. Patterson's bill is a brazen example of a lawmaker cutting off an entire market from hundreds of small businesses statewide.

FIGHTING BOOK BAN LEGISLATION
TEXAS FREEDOM FIGHTERS

Charley Rejsek never expected to be trawling the halls of the Texas State Capitol, let alone dressed as a mouse. Rejsek, at the time manager of Austin bookstore landmark Book People, had never before felt the need to be so political in her bookselling work. When I ask her about her efforts to oppose HB 900, she says, "I've protested, right? But I've never set up appointments and testified and stuff." But the brazenness of HB 900—"It was just so *wrong*"—inspired her to action. Taking her lead from librarians she knew, she started to build a coalition. Rejsek tells me, "We created handouts with the librarians talking about how HB 900 affected us. And we put our talking points together and turned it into handouts that we could distribute to the legislators who are making these decisions." And how would it affect Rejsek's store? She says, "We wouldn't be able to work with schools in general, because we can't read and rate books, so then we're just banned from working with school districts [...] I have a whole warehouse, a schools warehouse that we run our school business out of that employs three people. So, it would remove jobs," in addition to a significant revenue stream.

While school sales aren't the most profitable part of Book People's business, Rejsek says they're crucial to building community relations, an essential part of any bookstore's work. Therefore, HB 900 was a direct attack on the heart of what Texas bookstores do. In addition to teaming up with libraries to trawl the capitol halls, Rejsek also teamed up with her regional bookselling association to design a session for their spring 2023 conference to provide a space for Texas booksellers to discuss the bill. Out of the session sprang a listserv to "send out calls to action, updates on the bill, etc." Rejsek tells me, "I still hear from some of those stores today, telling about their current struggles and asking how to overcome them." Book People also updated their iconic marquee sign to oppose the bill; when they posted it on social media, Rep. Patterson retweeted it with this caption:

> It's amazing how many want sexually explicit materials in the hands of unaccompanied minors. HB 900 (aka READER Act) doesn't even touch bookstores, online

retailers or public libraries. It simply removes explicit content from school libraries and increases parental controls.

Patterson's tweet was a lie in a few ways; first, the idea that the bill "doesn't touch bookstores" is laughable. Second, when was the last time you saw a representative publicly attacking an iconic local small business? As outrageous as the tweet was, that wasn't even the most absurd day of Rejsek's efforts to prevent HB 900 from passing. Thursday, April 27, 2023, was just a few days before Independent Bookstore Day. That meant it fell during Bookstore Spirit Week, whose Thursday dress-up theme was "dress like your favorite character day." Rejsek came to work dressed like the mouse from *If You Give a Mouse a Cookie.* That morning, she got a call from the Capitol: The Speaker of the House wanted to talk to Rejsek about her concerns. With no time to change out of her mouse costume, she rushed across town to the Capitol to meet with the Speaker. Walking the Capitol halls so dressed is one thing; getting snubbed was another entirely. Rejsek tells me, "But politics are what they are—after waiting four hours, we only got to speak to his education policy advisors." (If you give a politician an appointment, he's going to want to ignore you. If he ignores you, he's going to want to vote against your interests).

It's unlikely the meeting would've made a difference, anyway, as Patterson had provided an easy way for the legislature to score political points without adding any work to the government's plate, since the bill pinned all the work on booksellers and librarians. And so, despite the best efforts of Rejsek alongside booksellers and librarians statewide, the READER Act passed on June 13, 2023. Almost immediately, Rejsek called American Booksellers Association CEO Allison Hill and asked, "What now?" Hill replied, "Give me a few days." And a few days later Hill called back to tell Rejsek the news: The ABA wanted Rejsek to sue the state of Texas.

Joining Rejsek as a co-plaintiff on the ABA's lawsuit would be Valerie Kohler, owner of Blue Willow Books in Houston. Rejsek and Kohler are something of a study in contrasts: In conversation, Rejsek is cool and calculated in what she says, while Kohler traffics in folksy anecdotes and loquacious charm. Rejsek is not a parent, Kohler brings up her kids several times as we talk. Rejsek started at Book People in 2019, while Kohler started at Blue Willow in 1996. Kohler is still at Blue Willow; in 2025, Rejsek left bookselling for a job directing a nonprofit focused on increasing literacy and book access among underserved youth.

Rejsek's former store is a massive modern superstore in the middle of Texas's most liberal city. In fact, Book People is Texas's largest independent bookstore. Blue Willow, on the other hand, is a small store in a Houston strip mall, wedged into a neighborhood that doesn't automatically support what they do politically. But regardless of their differences, they both stepped into a public (and more political than usual, at least for them) role fighting HB 900.

Kohler, enthusiastic and chatty, is a lifelong Houstonian. After a brief sojourn in California for her husband's job, the two returned to Houston and book lover Kohler quickly got a job at Blue Willow's predecessor store in her neighborhood. Soon after starting, the store's owner found herself thinking about retiring because of health issues. She pinpointed Kohler as a worthy successor, and in 1996 Kohler took over. She's been an enthusiastic Houston bookseller ever since, assembling a crack team of book experts and solidifying the store's community ties. Kohler loves it. She says, "It fits me. Books and retail, having grown up in retail and fitting with books that I love, it just all worked out. And I've been very, very lucky. Kathy, Alice, the rest of the staff, they're just awesome." But never did Kohler imagine she'd become such a public face of the fight for the freedom to read. Even as the anti-book movement in Texas ramped up, Kohler didn't think she'd ever have to. Surely, she thought, the anti-book activity of reps Krause and Patterson was simply too outrageous to be true. She remembers reading about Krause's list in the paper and telling her staff about the "craziness." When HB 900 was introduced, Kohler says she "was the one that kept saying, this is not going to pass. Calm down people. Calm down. This is not going to pass." One of the reasons it seemed impossible to Kohler was the sheer amount of work it would take to read and rate every book they've ever sold to a school. She tells me, "We just said that that's impossible. We can't possibly read them all, and we don't even know if they're all in print anymore." Not only was it an impossible *amount* of work, it was impossible work, especially among the typically opinionated booksellers of Blue Willow. Kohler says, "We can't even agree within our staff, much less trying to agree statewide." The potential for disagreement on a book's rating under HB 900 is especially terrifying given the prospect of the state finding a bookstore's ratings inaccurate and thus banning that store from ever selling to schools again. But, ridiculous as it seemed, Kohler was soon involved in the fight to prevent HB 900 from passing. When I ask her how she got involved, she tells me, "People were already calling me names on social media. I'm too old for that." It turned out, even if she didn't want to enter the fight (she did), the fight came to her.

Houston is far from the liberal stronghold that Austin is. Kohler says, "The neighborhoods that I live in and that the store is in and that surround us are a real mixed bag. But by and large they're pretty conservative." In Houston, Krause and Patterson had many allies and supporters, and some of them targeted the jovial, queer-friendly bookstore around the corner. Kohler isn't even on social media, but the conservative attacks still found their way to her. She tells me, "I got screenshots from friends and neighbors who were like, did you know they were saying this about you? I answered, 'I don't care really. You could say all you want. I'm still going to be here on the corner selling books. I'm not going to stop selling books.'" As Kohler sees it, movements like Moms for Liberty and MAGA have a real foothold in her neighborhood, driving some people to go to lengths to harass her store. One person filed a FOIA request and found an invoice for Blue Willow's sale of eight copies of *Gender Queer* to an area school. The person posted the invoice online and called Blue Willow "sickos" who sold "porn" to schools (Kohler says to me, in an aside, "Once they get into high school, if you don't let them read whatever they want to read, they're reading it on their phone in the hallway. There's more porn in the hallway than there is in the library.") The irony of this whole "sicko" *Gender Queer* situation? The school had ordered the copies of *Gender Queer* to evaluate a challenge of that title. If someone hadn't challenged that book, the school wouldn't have bought eight copies of it.

Texas Governor Greg Abbott signed HB 900 on June 13, 2023, and the bill was slated to go into effect on September 1. Kohler, Rejsek, and any other school-serving bookseller in Texas had two-and-a-half short months to prepare for the impossible: assigning sexual content ratings to every book they've ever sold to a school. In this desperate time for Texas booksellers, some reached out for help. While Rejsek was calling ABA CEO Allison Hill to ask, "What now?" Cathy Berner, a children's specialist at Blue Willow, and Megan Goel, former children's buyer at Book People, tracked down ABA CEO Hill at the 2023 Children's Institute conference in Milwaukee—held the week before the bill passed. Berner and Goel said to Hill, simply, "This bill is going to kill us." As Kohler tells it, that's the conversation that spurred the ABA into action: "That's where Allison was able to get some different organizations involved, Media Coalition and others. And so we sued the state of Texas." Days later, Hill phoned Rejsek, and the plaintiffs were lined up. Rather than prepare to enact this impossible law, the ABA, Kohler, and Rejsek instead prepared to take it down in the courts for the simple reason that it would be impossible to do business as usual under the law. Rejsek is quoted in a Texas Public Radio story saying, "The reason why we decided to sign on with this coalition of other bookstores, publishers, and authors now that it's law, is just because we just do not see a clear path forward in complying with the law as it's written."[145]

The lawsuit was filed in District Court in Austin on July 25. Its central argument hinges on the idea that HB 900 infringes on booksellers' freedom of speech. The introduction to the suit claims that HB 900 (which it calls, simply, "the Book Ban") "violates the First and Fourteenth Amendments to the U.S. Constitution because it is an overbroad and vague content-based law that targets protected speech and is not narrowly tailored to serve a compelling state interest. The Book Ban compels Plaintiffs to express the government's views, even if they do not agree, and operates as a prior restraint, two of the most egregious constitutional infringements." The lawsuit also addresses the fallout of the law, showing full awareness of the unofficial, silent book banning that comes with the anti-book atmosphere that a law like HB 900 creates:

> Indeed, the Book Ban's passage has already led to school districts halting the purchase of school library books. The full implementation of the Book Ban will cause a recall of many books in K-12 public schools, bans of even more, and the establishment of an unconstitutional—and unprecedented—state-wide book licensing regime that compels private companies and individuals to adopt the State's messages or face government punishment.

In response to the lawsuit, Jared Patterson, with characteristic subtlety, said in a statement, "To those standing against Texas schoolchildren I simply say, bring it with everything you have because I don't want to hear any excuses when we put the final nail in the coffin of your woke agenda."[146] I'll pause here to reiterate that, while I wanted to ask Patterson about this, he ignored my repeated interview requests.

Working against the September 1 deadline, things moved quickly. On August 31, the day before the law was set to go in effect, Federal District Judge Alan D. Albright issued a temporary injunction blocking the entire law from going into effect. Then, on September 25, The U.S. Court of Appeals for the Fifth Circuit issued an injunction blocking the injunction that blocked the law from going into effect—essentially reversing the stay and letting the bill become law, at least temporarily, until the case was settled. While the book-rating portion of the law remained in question thanks to the ongoing arguments in the case, Texas did begin drafting new standards for school libraries in accordance with provisions in HB 900.

Then in January, the Fifth Circuit issued a preliminary injunction, siding with the Plaintiffs on the book-rating portion of HB 900 but leaving the library standards intact. In defense of the book-rating portion of the READER Act, one of the state's arguments was that the book-rating system wasn't mandatory; nobody would be forced to comply with the book rating system, since bookstores don't *have* to sell to schools. The Fifth Circuit disagreed, writing:

> We are not persuaded. Plaintiffs allege that they will be harmed if they comply with READER and harmed if they don't. If Plaintiffs try to comply, they have alleged that it will cost them potentially millions of dollars to rate and review books. And if they don't comply, the law at least facially prohibits them from selling any books to schools—which would cost [plaintiff] Blue Willow nearly 20 percent of its revenue. These are concrete, cognizable injuries sufficient to confer standing, and the fact that the vendors are not required to participate in the program does not change that.[147]

During the suit, the State of Texas also argued that the ratings are simply factual information, like food nutrition labels. The Fifth Circuit shot that down, too, saying,

> We disagree. The ratings READER requires are neither factual nor uncontroversial. The statute requires vendors to undertake contextual analyses, weighing and balancing many factors to determine a rating for each book. Balancing a myriad of factors that depend on community standards is anything but the mere disclosure of factual information. And it has already proven controversial.[148]

In addition to all this, the Fifth Circuit also seemed quite receptive to the plaintiff's free speech arguments. In all, it was a resounding defeat for the book banners of the Texas government.

After the clear loss, the State of Texas appealed to the Fifth Circuit Court of Appeals. In April 2024, the panel of judges declined to reconsider the ruling. Patterson was again livid, saying, "It's incredibly disappointing that a majority of the 5th Circuit Court of Appeals sided with book vendors who push pornography on unsuspecting children in our public schools."[149] The last chance for the State of Texas was to send the ruling to the U.S. Supreme Court. For that to happen, Texas Attorney General Ken Paxton would have to file the appeal. In the wake of the appeal's failure, Jared Patterson urged Paxton to do so. Paxton had a July 15, 2024, deadline to do so. July 15, 2024, came and went with no announcement from Paxton. Turns out, there might have been a political problem for Patterson. In 2024, Paxton survived an impeachment attempt that found only two Republican state senators voting to convict him. But in the House, 70 percent of his fellow Republicans voted to convict, including Jared Patterson. This spicy bit of Texas politics might have been the death knell for the book-rating portion of HB 900. Rejsek tells me, "I think that this lawsuit kind of got caught up in politics because Patterson voted to impeach Paxton [...] And our attorney general was the one who would've had to send it to the Supreme Court. And so, I think that he didn't [submit the case to the Supreme Court] as a slap on the wrist to Patterson for voting for him to be impeached." Whatever kind of political maneuvering it took, the book-rating portion of HB 900 certainly seemed dead. Then, in October 2025, the final nail in the coffin: A federal judge in Waco ruled the book rating portion of HB 900 unconstitutional, making permanent the temporary injunction blocking the law and delivering a decisive win for Kohler, Rejsek, and the ABA. On Facebook, Rejsek called it "the best news ever" and "a huge win for the First Amendment, bookstores and the youngest readers in Texas!"

But Jared Patterson isn't one to accept defeat: Rejsek tells me, "Patterson tweeted that' he'd come back harder next session [...] he already has more book banning stuff in the works." As stated at the end of the last chapter, newly filed laws for the 2025 session include Patterson's HB 267, which would revise the Texas Penal Code to enable the criminal prosecution of librarians and booksellers for providing "material that is harmful to children." When combined with the prospect of SB 88, which eliminates the Miller Test so materials can more easily be declared obscene or harmful, Patterson's new tactic is terrifying. Neither bill made any progress during the 2025 Texas legislative session, but even the fact that these were introduced is alarming enough. Plus, one bill that did pass was Texas SB 13, which gives far-right parents a clear path to directly overseeing the curation of school libraries. Patterson and his ilk are tireless in their pursuit of curbing the right to read.

It's also worth noting that HB 900 is just one of dozens of laws in dozens of states aiming to restrict the right to read. In Arkansas, Florida, Iowa, Missouri, and elsewhere, being a librarian is being criminalized, access to books is being restricted, and far-right politicians are incorrectly labelling books about teenage sexuality or queer experiences as "pornography." For every successful lawsuit, there are many more laws that go into effect undisturbed. Thank goodness Kohler and Rejsek are in Texas to fight; may they inspire others across the country.

Both Kohler and Rejsek refuse to fully assume the mantle of Public Defender of Books, slipping out of any grandiose view of themselves as the national crusaders against book bans that they are. When I ask Rejsek about the lawsuit she tells me, "All the lawsuit is to me is time and anxiety" while holding up a huge pile of papers she's sorting through for discovery. Indeed, imagine what a talented bookseller like Rejsek could accomplish if Rep. Patterson hadn't forced her to shift so much time to fighting his restrictive bill. Down in Houston, Kohler makes sure to emphasize to me that "they didn't want us anywhere near the courtroom at any point." To her, the real advocacy is in her store among the people in her neighborhood. She tells me that Texas's efforts at book banning, and the lawsuit, come up in the store "every day." It's a strange role for her, who used to pride herself on being a "middle of the road" bookseller. She says, "If you've known me for any length of time, not until this time did I ever talk about politics in the store. And I made it perfectly clear to my staff, we don't talk politics here [...] this has kind of forced me out a little bit. I didn't know that was in me." Indeed, she relishes these conversations. To her, that's where the real work gets done. She tells me:

> My hope is that all the stores continue to just talk to their customers, I think is the most important thing. Without getting too belligerent, just one-on-one: "This is what we think here in the store. This is how we act in the store. This is how we sell in the store." I think that's the only way we can get to these people is keep talking to our customers [...] friend to friend, neighbor to neighbor, parent to parent, whatever it takes, speak on that level.

Kohler has found some success with this strategy. Despite a neighborhood that doesn't always agree with them, and a state that's actively fighting what they do best, Blue Willow continues to be a place for young readers to connect with all kinds of books.

Still, there's no replacing a school library, especially in a place like Houston. Sometimes the school library could be the only place kids can access books. Kohler says,

> I've seen a lot of posts from authors that say, "Hey, they can always get it at the local bookstore." Well, a lot of kids don't have access to the local bookstore. They don't even have access to the local library. Houston is so spread out that they'd have to take the bus and then they'd have to take another bus. Our big city urban school district has closed most of their libraries. That's the part that hurts my heart: The kids that are not going to have access to current books. They won't have the next *Wimpy Kid.* They won't have the next *Dog Man.* And it's just quite frankly sad.

Kohler is fighting an uphill battle in macro and micro. She sued the state of Texas, yes. But she's also trying to win hearts and minds one at a time, bookseller to customer, person to person, and even mother to mother. She's one person fighting against an intellectual chill. After all, it's not so much the book bans as the climate of fear inspired by book bans that's limiting kids' access to books. Kohler says, "I've heard all the stories about the librarians and the administrators coming through the libraries and pulling the books off the shelf without anybody even challenging them, just 'get 'em off the shelf because we don't want challenges.' It's kind of that quiet pull. I see these quiet pulls of books off the shelves, and I'm just trying to do one tiny little part."

WRITING THE BOOK ON BOOK BANS

On August 20, 2024, Philomena Polefrone stood in the crowd at the King's Theater in Brooklyn. She was there to see the Indigo

Girls and Melissa Etheridge, and to blow off steam during a busy and stressful time at work. The Indigo Girls took the stage for their set amidst a roar from the crowd. The lights came up revealing a huge banner behind them. The banner looked like a bookshelf. Polefrone, being a bookish person, of course squinted to read the titles of the books. *The Poet X. The Hate U Give. Crank. Me and Earl and the Dying Girl. Of Mice and Men. The Kite Runner. The Color Purple.* "Oh my god," Polefrone thought to herself. "Those are all banned books. I can't escape." Indeed, the job that Polefrone was trying to take a break from is this: overseeing the banned books initiative for the American Booksellers Association. She literally wrote the book on fighting book bans, and she couldn't even escape at an Indigo Girls show.

As we've seen in this book's introduction, Polefrone was devastated to lose a beloved and welcoming high school teacher—along with the safe space that teacher created—to a book ban spat at the high school she went to. From that day on, book bans became "a really personal issue for me actually, because [that teacher] was run out of the school." The idea remained in her head as she entered college and then grad school, where she eventually earned a PhD after writing a dissertation "on literature and activism, specifically the loop of those things reinforcing each other." While the activism in question was more environmental and anti-capitalist than pro right-to-read, Polefrone's fired teacher was always in her mind, especially as the book ban craze of 2022 and 2023 ramped up. At the same time, Polefrone was working as a lecturer in New York City when she ultimately found that "academia can't love you back." While considering a career pivot, a former student put Polefrone in touch with the American Booksellers Association's CEO, Allison Hill. What began as an informal kind of introduction quickly became a job interview as the two "really hit it off" around the subject of book bans. Hill mentioned that the ABA was looking to expand its advocacy team, and Polefrone soon became the organization's point person on the banned books issue.

Though major book ban lawsuits had been filed in Texas and Arkansas before Polefrone started, she soon took over management of those and the ABA's other anti-book ban initiatives. She started at the ABA on a Friday, and by the following Monday she was on the train to a regional booksellers' association conference. At the show, Polefrone had many conversations with booksellers. The conversations shaped her approach in the work she was commencing. She tells me, "It's no exaggeration to say that my sense of what needed to be done and what I needed to be doing came from talking to dozens if not hundreds of booksellers." She continues:

> I heard about booksellers who were seeing things happen in school boards around them and in their state legislatures that they, as booksellers, didn't know how to engage in. They were horrified by it, and they definitely understood that in a general way, it constituted a threat to bookselling because nobody thinks that book banners want to stop with schools and libraries. And I heard a lot of fear and trepidation about HB 900 or the READER Act in Texas. HB 900 really loomed large in everyone's mind.

Polefrone's first year showed some progress on the issue, especially in a legislative sense: She tells me that in the year since HB 900 was introduced, "three copycat bills were introduced in New Hampshire, South Carolina and Georgia; they all failed. I like to think that we had something to do with that. In fact, I know that we did." Still, there was much uncertainty about what to do, especially since the scale of the problem was so massive. Polefrone says, despite the failure of HB 900 copycat bills, that "there was this sense that nobody knew where it was going to stop. And in some cases just weren't sure, given the scale of a problem, what the most effective way to engage was." As Polefrone roamed the regional show floor with Hill, she says, "One of us used the word toolkit, and this is where my first big project at ABA came from." And so, the American Booksellers Association Right to Read Toolkit was born.

Part of the reason the Right has so successfully taken over school boards and spread their book-banning gospel is that they're using the same tactics everywhere. From Arkansas to Florida to Texas to Utah, the same groups spur people to positions of power in the same way. They have clear-cut strategies that they share among themselves: how to ban a book, how to take over a school board, how to hide books you don't approve of in libraries or bookstores. Polefrone's ABA Right to Read Toolkit was her first attempt at bringing such a game plan to the side of the folks defending books. It was necessary because, as Polefrone says, there is a "sense of increased hostility in bookstores. But there is also this sense that bookstore owners need to provide their employees with some kind of guidance in how to handle it, because suddenly [the hostility in question] was just the reality of bookselling." And so, a toolkit. The final product, available as a PDF on the ABA's website, is "meant as a way to cover as many of these different areas as possible. Here's how to write an op-ed for your paper, but also here's how to try to run a safe event." In the time since the toolkit was released, Polefrone has started posting weekly interviews with booksellers impacted by the assault on books, bringing those stories to a bigger audience. And then, after all this work, it became apparent that Polefrone could do one thing to reach an even bigger audience and give booksellers even more tools to fight back: She was going to write the book on fighting book bans.

Released in September 2024, the *ABA Right to Read Handbook* is the definitive practical guide to book bans and how to fight them. The idea, again, came from discussions with Allison Hill. The question at the time was this: What would a consumer version of the Banned Book Toolkit look like? Again, the idea was to create a game plan for the pro-book resistance just like the anti-book crusaders had. Polefrone says, "Because we're organizing against people who already have this hymn sheet that they've been singing from. And now we have the blueprint, and it's possible to use that blueprint to then push back against it. It's like they just left the plans of the Death Star just lying around, and here we are."

The *ABA Right to Read Handbook* is about as good a hymn sheet as you could imagine for the right-to-read resistance. If you're looking for an extremely practical, useful guide to fighting back against book bans in your community, put this book down and go pick up the *ABA Right to Read Handbook*. Though it has a lot of context, background, and interviews, at heart it's a step-by-step resource; early in the book a section called "Playbook: Using this Handbook in a Hurry" advises, "Need to hit the ground running with this handbook? Don't have time and history for context right now? We get it. Here are some sections to get you started."[150] And there's lots of practical advice about what to do, including guides to writing an op-ed, attending a school or library board meeting, and giving testimony at a government hearing. Perhaps most useful is a section how to tell a good book challenge policy from a bad one: For instance, good policies keep the right to challenge "limited to stakeholders," while bad policies allow anyone to challenge a book, which "has allowed a handful of individuals to create a book challenge crisis nationwide."[151] The *Handbook*'s practical nature is not to say that the contextual material isn't useful, though. The book starts with the most concise summary I've seen of the history of censorship in the United States. It also features interviews with important characters in the book ban resistance, including authors who have had their books banned. Many of these interviews are insightful; some are downright memorable, like Authors Against Book Bans organizer Maggie Tokuda-Hall, who says, "Just to give you a sense of how stupid this is, *Everyone Poops* has been removed [from a library in Huntington Beach, CA]. I'm not here to yuck anyone's yum, but if that's porn to you, that feels like a you issue, and you can just handle that privately. That doesn't need to be everybody's problem."[152] Polefrone is an excellent prose stylist, rendering complex issues in concise and clear terms and organizing the book in a way that fully enables actual use. I can't recommend the book enough; it's an invaluable resource. It's also a major sign of how seriously the bookstore industry is taking this crisis. Though libraries are the current target more often than not, there's nothing to say that bookstores aren't next, as evidenced by Jared Patterson's activity during the 2025 Texas legislative session.

BEACONS OF TOLERANCE

In the grand spirit of Lawrence Ferlinghetti, some booksellers are taking proactive action instead of letting the problem come to them. The Lynx is perhaps the first Florida bookstore to open as a response to the state's book ban crisis. Bestselling author and three-time National Book Award finalist Lauren Groff, along with her husband Clay Kallman, decided that opening a bookstore was the best way to fight back against the terrifying wave of anti-intellectual activity and legislation in their adopted home state. Groff calls the atmosphere in Florida right now an "icy breeze that's been blowing across Florida from the governor's mansion." The hostile climate for books, freedom of expression, and freedom of thought goes all the way to Ron DeSantis—much of the "icy breeze" has indeed been codified into legislation such as the infamous "Don't Say Gay" bill, among others. So, what can two people with one bookstore do to fight the wind?

Florida leads the country in book bans. According to a September 2023 PEN report, "More books were pulled from shelves in Florida public schools compared to any other state during the past school year."[153] In the year spanning June 2022 to July

2023, PEN tracked 3,362 book bans in public school classrooms and libraries, representing a 33 percent increase over the previous year. 1,400 of those bans—40 percent—happened in Florida. That's well more than double the bans reported in the second-place state, Texas.[154] The April 2024 PEN report shows Florida is again leading the pack with 3,135 bans—almost as much as the previous year's number for the entire country. Several pieces of legislation in Florida fuel this fire, such as 2022's "Parental Rights in Education" act, otherwise known as the "Don't Say Gay" bill. Recently expanded, the law prohibits discussions and teaching about gender identity and sexual orientation for all grades in Florida schools. Another law, HB 1069, requires all books in classroom or school libraries to be purchased by a certified media specialist—a position being cut from many schools due to budget cuts originating in, you guessed it, Ron DeSantis's state government. The same law requires all school libraries to create a searchable public directory of their collections. This places an expensive burden on already-stretched library workers. Also, of course, it opens libraries to public scrutiny via book challenges. Under the law, challenges don't even have to be successful to restrict access—according to *Politico*, any challenged book must be "pulled from shelves within five days and remain out of circulation for the duration of any challenge."[155] A book can only be reinstated after a public hearing is held to debate the book's merits. That's the "icy wind" Groff was referring to—even without a successful challenge, books can be taken from young readers via challenge-based purgatory or even self-censorship by teachers and librarians. Thanks to HB 1069, anyone can search a Florida school library's collection and file a challenge, thus removing that book from circulation.

Predictably, the passage and implementation of HB 1069 led to significant resistance. For one thing, several major publishers and Florida parents filed a lawsuit challenging the bill in June

2024. The District Court for Florida dismissed the case in January 2025, but the plaintiffs filed an appeal in June 2025. Then, in August 2025, the court ruled in favor of the plaintiffs and the right to read by striking down significant parts of the law. Most notably, Judge Carlos E. Mendoza rejected the idea that any content dealing with sex is automatically pornographic, saying, "The Court must conclude that there is no constitutional application of a prohibition against books containing material that 'describes sexual conduct.'" In his eyes, the bill created an "I know it when I see it" standard for obscenity originating with individual parents, not officials or policy. This system would assign librarians the impossible task of guessing what books parents might object to. Of course, the application of this system would lead to an icy climate of self-censorship, which is perhaps the whole point, but it's an idea that Mendoza's ruling rejects. Additionally, Mendoza rejected Florida's claim that bulk removal of school library books is protected government speech. He writes, "slapping the label of government speech on book removals only serves to stifle disfavored viewpoints." The decision is not a complete repeal of the law, yet it represents another striking court win for the freedom to read. A statement on behalf of the plaintiff group states, "This is a sweeping victory for the right to read, and for every student's freedom to think, learn, and explore ideas" Of course, the state appealed and as this book goes to print, the results of that appeal are not yet determined. Regardless of whether the state's appeal succeeds, the fight isn't just in the courtrooms; some folks are answering the Florida book ban mayhem with mayhem of their own. Lauren Groff and Clay Kallman are two of those people.

The Lynx bookstore sits on South Main Street in downtown Gainesville, Florida. The front of the building is overwhelmed by a massive mural of the store's sneering feline namesake. Above the lynx's tail is the store's motto: "Watch us bite back." It's a perfect summation of the operating spirit of Groff's team at The

Lynx. Like many authors, Groff had dreamed of what it would be like to have a bookstore. But she and her husband were driven to action by Ron DeSantis's "icy breeze;" In May 2024, Groff told *The New York Times*, "This store would probably still be a pipe dream if the book bans hadn't happened . . . I don't want to live in a place where we stifle free expression."[156]

One of the factors behind The Lynx's early success is of course the presence of Groff herself—a beloved author opening a bookstore to fight book bans is a good story. But credit is also due to Groff's adopted hometown: She tells me, "The thing is, Gainesville is super punk and it's very hippie. We're already a culture of resistance and subversion in the middle of a state like Florida." But rather than become a silo, sealed off from what's going on in the rest of the state, Groff and team are taking advantage of Gainesville's local support to become a home base for efforts elsewhere. She considers Gainesville "a very, very dark blue center of the state from which we can push into the external counties and actually do things and to create almost a beacon of tolerance. That's what we wanted the bookstore to be, a beacon of tolerance." Part of being a beacon of tolerance, to Groff, is to give away what she calls "Dolly Parton levels" of banned books. Part of it is to be a noisy advocate presence on social media. Part of it is to highlight and sell banned books in-store. But at its core, the root of being a beacon of tolerance is to simply be a safe place in a state that's short on them. Groff says, "If you get a day to come into Gainesville, beautiful transgender people who are terrified for your lives out in Marion County, you can spend the day in the store and just sit there if you want to because we are a third space for you." Through all this work, Groff is hoping to both fight authoritarianism in Florida, and also to fight the image that everyone in Florida is a fascist. Of course, from its inception the store has been deeply rooted in fighting the icy breeze of fascism in Florida. But also, as Groff tells me, "There is a profound symbolism of being a place of resistance that is visible and loud and at the very heart of the state. I want to change the narrative and be like, 'Actually, no, there are tons of really good people doing a lot of really good things in Florida.'"

The balance between fighting creeping authoritarianism and battling statewide generalizations is an important one (and one I certainly recognize from my years of advocacy and organizing in Kansas). In my conversation with her, Groff is quick to highlight the breadth of Florida anti-book ban work beyond her efforts at The Lynx. When I suggest the book ban situation is a silent crisis, she strongly rebukes me: "In Florida it's not silent at all." She mentions PEN America's anti-book ban work from their dedicated Florida office, which organized a Unified Voices against Book Bans summit in early 2024. Groff was there. "We heard a great deal from everyone, from not only librarians and schoolteachers, but people in the community, the parents who are actually fighting back and politicians and artists. We heard from everybody. So I actually think, at least on the ground here, it's definitely not silent." Hearing from everybody is key to her organizing strategy—it's not just about running a bookstore that bites back, it's about coalition building. Groff tells me,

> I think there really is a coalition forming and it's really strong and it's really bold. And I think libraries, librarians, and schoolteachers really feel like there is a mass of people at their backs. I mean, in Florida, 85 percent of the populace thinks book bans are stupid [...] so having a coalition, a really strong coalition, not just the booksellers, but of everyone that's actually sort of stopping the chill in its tracks. I think in a lot of ways it's giving people a lot of strength to resist. And that makes me feel really excited about where we're going to go with this.

Broad, coalition-based resistance is vital to the issue of book bans because, of course, it's not just about book bans. Many on the right are using book bans (and the culture wars in general) as a kind of smoke screen to advance their broader cultural goals, like kneecapping public education and eliminating the separation between church and state. Groff says,

> These book bans are the start of a very bad downward slide. Every modern genocide has started with book burning. This is absolutely the truth. At the same time, these book bans are sort of like a frenzy, a set of fireworks thrown up by the right wing so that other, even more severe, authoritarian things can take place under the cover of night or under the cover of our distraction.

Hence the need to bite back. Book bans are bad, but they're also a sign of even more nefarious work. And even if things get even worse, Groff is ready to put herself on the line. She tells me, with conviction,

> I do think it's possible we will come to a point with the emboldening of the authoritarian forces that booksellers will be legally responsible for the books that they're selling in the store. And if that's the case, then I'm very willing to be a target personally, to be the person who gets arrested for selling gay books. If Ron DeSantis and his goons come get me, I have a very big microphone.

If you ask me, this is exactly what the fight against book bans needs in order to evolve from a silent crisis to a nationwide reckoning: a beloved author with mighty little bookstore and a big microphone willing to put herself on the line to protect freedom of expression and try to prevent the fight against books from becoming the fight against even more. Thank goodness Groff and team are fighting back in Florida, and thank goodness their message is going national.

A famous author opening a bookstore as a direct challenge to Ron DeSantis is bound to be a big story. According to *The New York Times*, the store's opening brought a flood of donations from across the country. That's after the store raised $116,000 on Indiegogo in preparation for its launch. Support has come in non-monetary forms, too, including from other author-booksellers. In opening the store, Groff consulted with Emma Straub, *New York Times* bestselling author and owner of Brooklyn's Books are Magic. Straub made a point to help Groff focus on the surprising yet pragmatic details of bookselling: She says, "A lot of us authors don't spend that much time thinking about that part. We think about the books and the community, all of that big picture stuff, and we don't necessarily think about the nuts and bolts, retail-ness of it. Like, oh by the way, you need a mop."[157]

The national support for The Lynx opening extends to its political work as well. In July 2024, Books Are Magic announced the Banned Book Distribution Network, a fundraising initiative to support The Lynx's work in Florida. Straub was already on high alert about books and school libraries. In 2023, she published the extremely cute and deeply uncontroversial picture book *Very Good Hats*. Part of her tour for the book had her visiting a few elementary schools in book ban capital—and home of Cameron Samuels—Katy, Texas. But before the visit could happen, a Katy parent found a Tweet from 2022 where Straub writes, "Fuck guns, fuck people who care more about controlling women's bodies than protecting all of us from people with guns, fuck! It's too much. So heartbroken." That single tweet, and a complaint from that lone parent, was enough to cancel Straub's visit to Katy. Straub told *School Library Journal*, "Was I going to swear at these children? Was I going to talk about guns? No. I was going to read a picture book about hats."[158] The whole experience "really showed me how this works," Straub says of the reactionary modern-day politics of children's libraries. Surely the incident was in Straub's mind as her friend Lauren Groff was in Florida getting The Lynx off the ground.

The Banned Book Distribution Network started in earnest when, even in her native deep-blue Brooklyn, Straub began to feel the encroachment of the far right's anti-book campaigning. For one thing, in March 2024, a dumpster outside Staten Island's PS55 school was found filled with discarded books. The books, most of which had LGBTQ+ characters or authors, were stamped with the phrase "not approved." Some even had sticky notes on them adorned with phrases like "Not approved. Discusses dad being transgender," "Teenage girls having a crush on another girl in class," or "negative slant on white people" on a book about Native American history.[159] Then, mere weeks later, a Manhattan Community Education Council—a type of liaison between the public and the city department of education—passed a resolution targeting trans athletes. Seeing that nowhere was safe, even her beloved New York City, Straub leapt into action. She tells me, "I don't have time to create some new organization, but I definitely have time to collect funds and then give it to someone else. And so I thought, 'Okay, who's doing banned book stuff in Florida who I already love? And so I called Lauren and I was like, basically, who should I give money to? Should I give money to you?" Groff said yes, and so two of the country's most famous bookseller-authors teamed up to turn Florida's attacks on the freedom to read into a national issue. In the time since that partnership, The Lynx has gone even further in solidifying its commitment to fighting Florida's icy breeze. In 2024, Groff founded The Lynx Watch, a 501(c)(3) nonprofit spinoff of the bookstore that's exclusively devoted to distributing free copies of banned books in Florida.

From Florida to Texas, from Staten Island to Utah, booksellers find themselves on the front lines of the attack on the freedom to read. But they also have found ways to fight back. Drag Story Hour is helping booksellers and organizers learn the standards of community safety plans. A Utah drag queen and bookseller is risking her personal safety to provide safe places for LGBTQ folks. A beloved author opened a bookstore in direct defiance of her state government's attack on books, and another beloved author is helping her raise enough money to give away "Dolly Parton amounts" of banned books. And in Texas, two booksellers led the charge to defeat a brutally restrictive state law that threatened bookstores' very ability to succeed. It's no mistake that these efforts are coming from bookstores, much like City Lights' efforts to protect *Howl*. A bookstore is a particularly nimble weapon in this fight, untethered to any right-wing takeovers of public policy or funding. Ironically, the same unjust laws that allow bakers to deny service to queer couples allow places like The Lynx to fight back against the right-wing politicians who dream up such violent policy in the first place. Groff tells me,

> That's why we opened a private bookstore, because we don't have to take any state money. We can actually put up a big sign with Ron DeSantis's face and devil horns on it if we want to. We can do that. I mean, this is the right wing's playgrounds, right? We're joining them in their playground on purpose, because that's also a tool. It's very intentional.

In a real way, a bookstore is enough outside the system that it's free to act as a beacon of resistance, a kind of small rebel base where attacks on the system can be launched. For now, at least. And good thing, because the system is big, violent, and entrenched. The libraries and public institutions need all the help they can get.

☛ HOW TO DEFEND BOOKS

MAKE A PLAN TO PROTECT THE MOST VULNERABLE

In the midst of the far right's assault on books and diverse identities, it's more important than ever to provide safe spaces and programming for vulnerable populations. Unfortunately, that same assault makes doing that work more dangerous than ever. It's important to plan ahead and ensure those spaces stay safe, even in the face of right-wing attacks. I'll note that involving law enforcement is not always going to make things safer, as some members of vulnerable populations may be made more vulnerable by the presence of police. Instead, rely on good community organizing and resources to make a plan to keep everyone safe.

USE YOUR RESOURCES

You don't have to do this alone. Philomena Polefrone has written an invaluable resource in the *ABA Right to Read Handbook*, full of detailed instructions and strategies for fighting book bans. Drag Story Hour's safety plan is thorough and useful. Organizations like the American Booksellers Association and others in this book's appendix are here to ensure book ban victims are not alone. If you try to reinvent the wheel, you'll find yourself overwhelmed and outmaneuvered by the right. Good thing there are an ever-increasing amount of resources to help this crisis' victims.

TAKE LEGAL ACTION

Though the courts are not always the fastest or best way to solve a crisis like this, they may be useful in stopping some book banning activity, as in the case of Valerie Kohler and Charley Rejsek's HB 900 lawsuit in Texas. An emerging theme of the book ban crisis is that a lot of these book ban bills don't stand up in court. At least so far, the Miller Test has stood, and many judges see these bills as the blatant First Amendment violations they are.

One note: legal work is expensive, and the right's flood-the-zone strategy can easily lead the book ban opposition to quickly be outspent and drained of resources. Even if you're not at the heart of a book ban situation, you can always donate to those who are.

CHAPTER 4: "A SYMBOL OF THE RESISTANCE": PALESTINE

*A*s bad as the American book banning is, especially paired with the broader wave of Christian nationalism, it is far from the only contemporary instance of the political and religious right attacking certain identities via their books and stories. If we look beyond libraries, schools, and bookstores, we can see how widespread the problem is, and indeed what it looks like if this anti-book and anti-diversity assault is taken to even further extremes. What does the endgame of this assault on stories and identities look like? International book ban crises may hold the answer. From Ukraine to Hong Kong, authors, readers, librarians, and booksellers are coming under attack. Nowhere is that more true than in Palestine during Israel's assault in the wake of Hamas's nightmarish October 7, 2023, attack on Israeli citizens. The resulting genocidal attack on Gaza has led to a catastrophic loss of Palestinian life but also a devastating loss of Palestinian culture, writing, and stories. Paired with the genocidal military attack is a quieter but no less brutal wave of attacks on Palestinian identity through stories and books. It is here we will turn to explore a worst-case scenario of what the book ban movement might be capable of.

MOSAB ABU TOHA

Paul Yamazaki, protégé of Shig Murao and 50-year veteran bookseller at City Lights, suggests that we go to Café Zoetrope for a bite and a drink. Café Zoetrope, a block away from City Lights, is Francis Ford Coppola's old-school Italian bistro. Here's how much of an icon Yamazaki is in North Beach: he has his own table at Zoetrope. The entire population of San Francisco (and the world) is prohibited from sitting there, unless they're a guest of Mr. Yamazaki. As we enter the cluttered and charming space, a waiter greets Yamazaki by name and leads us to his corner booth. Waitstaff are greeted, menus are perused, drinks are ordered, and Yamazaki and I proceed to discuss City Lights' legacy. I ask him how the *Howl* trial resonates today and how City Lights is continuing that work. Sipping his sparkling wine, he tells me the *Howl* trial and its legacy are a question of using books to open up doors into new and unknown rooms of understanding. It's a metaphor he returns to again and again throughout our conversation, perhaps inspired by his bookstore's series of little rooms. When discussing the origin of *Howl*, he tells me, "Lawrence immediately recognized both the literary qualities in *Howl*, but he also recognized the potentiality of really broadening cultural understanding. Even today, with people reading *Howl* for the first time. It opens a lot of doors." Pizza arrives and Yamazaki absolutely insists I have some, refusing to continue our conversation until I have a piece. Satisfied as I take a bite, he weighs in on today's wave of book challenges and bans. To him, it's all an "attempt to take us back two centuries," adding that the fear of dissenting speech is nothing new—it pre- and post-dates *Howl* all the way back to the beginning of America. He tells me, "We've always had this conflict, even before there were 13 states. It's all the same: the Comstock Act, the Scopes Monkey Trial. It's all just shutting down knowledge. To me, this is still a question: Why are people so afraid? I don't know the answer to that."

Pizza eaten, wine drunk, we return to City Lights to finish the tour. We walk through the sunny fiction room, through a little annex, and up a staircase and into the poetry room. This is probably my favorite part of any bookstore in the world, a hushed sanctuary bursting with slim poetry volumes and warm sunlight. I could spend hours here (in fact, I do, returning the day after my interview with Yamazaki). Yamazaki points to the small window (above "the poet's chair," according to a painted sign in Lawrence Ferlinghetti's handwriting). The window has a view of a terraced and hodgepodge collection of rooftops, a dense urban view. Yamazaki tells me that the view reminded Ferlinghetti of New York, and that's why wanted to add this room to the meandering footprint of City Lights. Next to the window is a small table with a framed photo of a young, bearded man. Next to the photo is a stack of small purple books. It has the feel of a shrine—especially poignant since the whole poetry room already feels like a shrine. It's a shrine within a shrine. The author to whom the shrine is dedicated, Mosab Abu Toha, as well as his City Lights-published book, *Things You May Find Hidden in My Ear*, is perhaps the clearest example of City Lights continuing the story that began with the publication of *Howl*.

Elaine Katzenberger has been the editor of the publishing side of City Lights since 2007, but she's worked there for much longer. Her City Lights origin story is typical: She was bartending at Vesuvio's next door, got sick of it, knew a bookseller at City Lights who convinced her to come work there, wasn't sure it was a permanent thing, ended up there for decades, and now runs the place. One of her duties as City Lights's publisher, of course, is to act as custodian of the legendary Pocket Poets series. When I ask her what makes a Pocket Poets book, she says it's simple: "It's got to be revolutionary." Perhaps this is what crossed her mind when she first read Mosab Abu Toha's poetry in the spring of 2021, as Israeli bombs rained down on Gaza.

Mosab Abu Toha was born in 1992 in the al-Shati refugee camp west of Gaza City. His father was born in the same camp, and his mother was born in Jabalia, "the largest refugee camp in Gaza, and in the world."[160] As a kid, it didn't really strike him that he was being raised as a refugee; he writes, "I never realized I was born in a refugee camp because that was just my world. I mean, a fish doesn't ask: why don't we walk on the street and go shopping?"[161] To him, the first sign of the violence shaping his world happened when he was eight, watching "an Apache helicopter shoot a rocket into a building."[162] Of course, even in a warzone there was room for poetry, and Abu Toha was immersed from an early age. He began writing poetry after enrolling at the Islamic University of Gaza, where he fell in love with studying English grammar. When he was one month away from graduating, "the Israelis bombed the administration building of [...] the Islamic University of Gaza. The English department was destroyed. The many books resting on the shelves of my professors were just lying under the rubble of the building."[163] Amidst the death and destruction of Israel's repeated campaigns against Gaza, Abu Toha began to write poetry. Clear, frank poetry about not only the realities of living under constant Israeli assault, but also the beauty and humanity of the Palestinian people.

Eventually, the poems reached an editor friend of Elaine Katzenberger. As she tells it, "He's the one who sent me a few poems. This was in the spring of 2021 when the bombing campaign was happening. Both of us were just really excited about them and we were like, 'Okay, we're doing a book. We're just going to make this happen.'" Even as Gaza was under assault and attention was focused there, publishing a Palestinian poet wasn't a sure bet for City Lights. Katzenberger tells me, "It's always been difficult for Palestinians to have their viewpoint and their voices heard. There's actually a great deal of access now [in the wake of October 7, 2023] whereas before, I think it'd be like, oh yeah, another poet in translation. Total snoozefest." It wasn't only the apathy of market forces that prevented Palestinian poetry from reaching a global audience; no doubt thanks to Israel's blockades of Gaza and the subsequent lack of resources, there have been long stretches of many years when no active publisher was creating books in Palestine.

I ask Katzenberger if she feared any pushback, and she shrugs me off, saying, "I didn't have any doubt that we would publish that book." And thank goodness; something about Abu Toha's work struck a chord with readers, even years before October 7 turned the world's attention to Gaza in a new way. Katzenberger attributes part of the poetry's appeal to Abu Toha's craft, "Mosab's work is very straightforward. I mean, it's beautifully crafted, but it's very accessible poetry." The book found some success, selling modestly well and winning a few awards, including the American Book Award. For Katzenberger, publishing Abu Toha's book was one small way to help as, across the ocean, Gaza was bombarded. She tells me, "When I published that book, it was 2022. I published Mosab in response to what seemed then one of the most brutal bombing campaigns that Israel had carried out for a while. [I had] this sense of giving voice to this person and putting a spotlight on how he's able to talk about this, as one way of helping." But, she adds, Abu Toha's work is not defined only by the trauma of living in Gaza. She explains,

> I'm not saying this to minimize at all what people are living through, but I will say Mosab never stopped writing poems. What I think Mosab's book shows is that for people growing up in Palestine, this is life. So life goes on and life goes on. For his entire life, it was one war situation after another. So it means people have families, they celebrate birthdays, they go to school, they write poems, they do all the things that other human beings do, and they get shot, and their houses get bombed, and all the other horrible things happen too. And I think actually

understanding that is important because otherwise it's just kind of dehumanizing people and turning them into a caricature of who they actually are.

In short, if you can attack someone's identity by attacking their stories, people can also create identity by telling stories. Ultimately, Katzenberger published Abu Toha's poems as an attempt to do one small thing to help humanize the Palestinian people as they were under a brutal attack. Then, two years later, an even more brutal assault on Gaza began. All of a sudden, the act of bearing witness to Palestinian voices grew much more urgent in the minds of many readers. People were turning to voices from Palestine, perhaps chief among them the young poet with the City Lights book.

In the wake of October 7, *Things You May Find Hidden in My Ear* found its way to even more readers. City Lights ordered reprint after reprint after reprint. Even more readers discovered Abu Toha through his prose dispatches from Gaza under siege. He plainly and clearly described the tragedy, grief, and challenge of navigating a warzone with his family. Dispatches appeared in *The Atlantic* and *The New Yorker* outlining his family's horrifying journey: evacuating their house only to learn later that it was destroyed by a bomb. Moving from a refugee camp to a crowded UNRWA school. Trying to keep his family safe and fed. The essays are heartbreaking: "In Gaza, a child is not really a child. Our eight-year-old son, Yazzan, has been talking about fetching his toys from the ruins of our house. He should be learning how to draw, how to play soccer, how to take a family photo. Instead, he is learning how to hide when bombs fall." A huge international audience got a glimpse into daily life in besieged Gaza thanks to Abu Toha's dispatches. Eventually, Abu Toha and family learned that they were on a list of names cleared to leave Gaza through the Rafah border crossing with Egypt. The journey south to the crossing was perilous, though, and multiple calamities delayed their trek. Then, in mid-November 2023, they finally set out.

Abu Toha and his family hired a donkey cart to take them south to the border. A few hours into the journey they came across an Israeli checkpoint, which the soldiers made by simply parking a tank sideways across the road. One of his sons was born in America, so Abu Toha held up his paperwork with the blue American passport facing outward. Despite living his entire life under Israeli occupation, Abu Toha writes, "These are the first Israeli soldiers I have seen. I am not afraid of them, but I will be soon."[164] An Israeli solider fired his gun into the ground to make a point. The crowd of Palestinian refugees grew restless and panicky. One of the Israeli soldiers had a megaphone and was shouting out arrest orders simply by describing people's appearances. Abu Toha explains what happened next: "They're not going to pull me out of the line, I think. I am holding Mostafa and flashing his American passport. Then the soldier says, 'The young man with the black backpack who is carrying a red-haired boy. Put the boy down and come my way.' He is talking to me."[165] Abu Toha joined a line of men waiting on their knees on the ground. And then, "After about a half hour, I hear my full name, twice: 'Mosab Mostafa Hasan Abu Toha.' I'm puzzled. I didn't show anyone my I.D. when I was pulled out of line. How do they know my name?"[166] It's a good question. It's hard to look at the statistics and think the Israeli army isn't targeting writers and journalists, and few Gazan writers were more visible than Abu Toha thanks to his dispatches in American magazines. According to the Committee to Protect Journalists, as of October 2025, at least 198 Palestinian journalists have been killed, with another 162 journalists injured, 2 reported missing, and 92 arrested.[167] For journalists, it is by far one of the deadliest warzones ever. One poet, the beloved Refaat Alareer, wrote a poem for his daughter called "If I Must Die" that became a popular commemoration of Palestinian grief, shared online and at protests around the world. Alareer was killed in an Israeli strike, and a few months later his daughter was too. Mosab Abu Toha had good reason to wonder why the Israeli army had his full name. Regardless, he was led past the tank and told to strip. He stood naked before Israeli soldiers joking in Hebrew. He writes, "This is the first time in my life that strangers have looked at me naked."[168] When he asked about his documents and the possibility of making it to the Rafah crossing, an Israeli soldier said, "Shut up, you son of a bitch."[169] They asked him if he was a part of Hamas, and he couldn't figure out how to convince the soldiers that he in fact wasn't. They beat him. Then, it became official: on November 19, 2023, Mosab Abu Toha was arrested and brought into Israeli custody.

As soon as she heard the news of Abu Toha's arrest, Elaine Katzenberger wondered how to spring into action. She tells me, "I already knew that were going to be a support network for Mosab." And a network it was—Katzenberger says, "City Lights wasn't the only institution that had been interested in him and his work in the States." People from all those places, including Harvard and Syracuse, where Abu Toha had studied, began a sprawling email thread to try to figure out what to do. Katzenberger describes it as "kind of organic. The email thread just kept adding more people, and it was all like, what do we do? What do we do? Okay, here, I'm doing this. What are you doing? And it just went like that." City Lights issued a statement "calling for the international community to demand the release of Mosab Abu Toha and all hostages and prisoners in Gaza and Israel." From *The Guardian* to *The Washington Post* to *Publishers Weekly*, reports of Abu Toha's arrest spread across the Internet. The story got big, much bigger than a small publisher trying to protect their poet. Katzenberger tells me, "It became pretty clear to me early that whatever clout or power that City Lights might have institutionally was actually quite small in comparison to some of the other people who were working on his behalf. So it wasn't like I was sanguine about what would happen to Mosab, but I could see that every possible lever was being pulled." Katzenberger was privy to efforts to help Mosab reaching all the way up to the U.S. Government: "It was interesting to understand who actually had the ear of the State Department," she tells me. Fairly rapidly, the outcry turned into a PR disaster for the Israeli army. Katzenberger figures that the IDF "realized pretty quickly that they had picked up the wrong guy, because this person had a lot of exposure and support, and they weren't going to get away with this so easily." After days of international outcry presumably invisible to the imprisoned poet, Mosab Abu Toha woke up to "a soldier [saying] something in English that I cannot believe. 'We are sorry about the mistake. You are going home.'"[170] Two days after he was arrested, Mosab Abu Toha was freed and reunited with his family. Eventually he was contacted by the U.S. Embassy in Jerusalem, who told him to head with his family to the Rafah crossing once again. They made it safely this time and successfully crossed into Egypt. It's hard to imagine that the international outcry didn't help Mosab Abu Toha's fate; Israel, already fast becoming a pariah state due to its horrific assault on Gaza, perhaps couldn't deal with the optics of arresting or killing a writer this beloved. But not everyone is as widely read, or as well-known in the English-speaking world, as Mosab Abu Toha. He writes, "I think about the words 'We are sorry about the mistake.' I wonder how many mistakes the Israeli Army has made, and whether they will say sorry to any-one else."[171] Elaine Katzenberger shares a similar thought as she reflects on the difficult time when nobody knew where her friend was: she tells me, "There are people who have never been heard from again, who might still be held or dead."

Long before he became a prominent Palestinian writer, before he was published in *The New Yorker*, before he studied at Harvard or Syracuse, Mosab Abu Toha was a university student standing in the rubble of the bombed administration building at the Islamic University of Gaza. It was August 2014, amid yet another Israeli bombing attack against Gaza. As he puts it, "One of the first things I saw shook me deeply—books buried under tons of concrete and dust. I had never imagined that books could be harmed so ruthlessly."[172] In the U.S., radical right-wing forces ban books. In Palestine, Israel bombs them. The first book Abu Toha delicately extracted from the rubble was the *Norton Anthology of American Literature*. He cried. He posted a picture of the Norton alongside a picture of his damaged home library on Facebook. People responded, sending messages of solidarity and support. And then, "a few months later, the idea occurred to me to create a public English-language library that everyone in Gaza could use."[173] Before he was a prisoner or a City Lights-published poet, Mosab Abu Toha was a librarian. With characteristic candor, Abu Toha writes:

> Everything we in Gaza had experienced—being bombed frequently and regularly cut off from electricity, but also deliberately deprived of culture through a shortage of libraries, library books, and access to vital informational resources abroad—made me a man of action. I no longer saw myself as just a Palestinian student of British and American literature, but as a librarian-in-the-making, determined to create a new library, an English-language library—something that did not exist in Gaza.[174]

And so began the efforts to build the Edward Said Memorial Library.

Abu Toha emailed anyone who could help, including Noam Chomsky. He created a Facebook page called "Library and Bookshop for Gaza." People from around the world sent books. Israel's blockade has made it impossible to this day to send international mail to a specific house in Gaza, so Abu Toha had people send books to what was left of the Islamic University. When the books arrived, university staff would call him, and he'd take a taxi to retrieve them. Once his apartment was full of books, he started to ask for money to buy furniture and rent a room. He was building Gaza's first English library from nothing but his own enthusiasm and a lot of social media outreach. He rented two small rooms in Beit Lahia, then a bigger, permanent home with "a reading room, a children's room, an arts room, and a lecture room."[175] That first branch opened in summer 2017, followed by a Gaza City branch in 2019. Like libraries in the United States, the Edward Said Memorial Libraries were designed to function as more than just book repositories. As Abu Toha writes, "Both libraries offer not only a venue for reading and borrowing books, but also a reading club, English club, English language lessons, music and drawing sessions, computer lessons in a lab, and a children's corner."[176] But the importance of the libraries extends even beyond their programming. Abu Toha writes, "In the aftermath of the frequent bombings in Gaza, many depressed and traumatized children come to the Edward Said libraries to seek psychological support from the staff. The two libraries care as much as possible for these children."[177] In creating his libraries, Mosab Abu Toha created community spaces through literary spaces.

Getting books into Gaza isn't easy. Early in the life of Abu Toha's libraries, Noam Chomsky sent a shipment of books. But at that time, in April 2016, Israel had stopped the flow of all mail into Gaza (as we'll see in the next chapter, preventing the mailing of books is a key move in the prison book banner's toolkit). Abu Toha writes, "I didn't think that the draconian Israeli ban would apply to books for children, linguists, and anyone interested in literature, but I was wrong. That confirmed to me that Israel was waging a deliberate and systematic attack on Palestinian learning by depriving the people of knowledge."[178] It took six months for Chomsky's books to arrive. Even when books did arrive, they were handled carelessly and exposed to the elements by Israeli armed forces. Other times, Abu Toha was told he'd have to travel to the West Bank to get shipments of books, which he says "is like asking the head of an American library to travel through Mexico to pick up a parcel in Guatemala."[179] The list of "Kafakaesque moments" Abu Toha faced in building his library is long—a fact that led him to realize that "knowledge gets restricted by the occupiers, so much that, because of the endless siege, a new book has become a luxury in Gaza. I often think about this impact of this on education, on the ability to think critically and creatively, and on the ability to envision a future."[180] One way this siege on knowledge manifests is in book bans—Israel "banned and confiscated 6,420 books between 1967 and 1995 in Gaza and the West Bank."[181] Throughout the history of Israel and its occupation of Palestine, up to 60 lists of banned books have represented over 1,600 titles. According to Abu Toha, people in Gaza "are not allowed to travel freely, even through books."[182]

Despite it all, Abu Toha did manage to create what he set out to create, and the branches of the Edward Said Memorial Library took their place in the Palestinian cultural firmament. Then came October 2023. When I interviewed her in spring 2024, Elaine Katzenberger told me that Abu Toha "is pretty sure that [the library] is gone." Still, a long time passed without any concrete news about the branches of the Edward Said Memorial Library. It simply wasn't safe enough for anyone to go check on them. One thing he did know was that he had lost a librarian—on December 7, 2023, Edward Said Memorial Library librarian Doaa Al-Masri was killed along with her whole family. The fate of the library itself wasn't known until much, much later, after an uneasy and temporary ceasefire arrived in January 2025. It was only then that the fate of the libraries was confirmed. Abu Toha delivered the devastating news on January 22, 2025, via Twitter. He wrote, "Today morning with a heavy heart I received the news of the destruction of the Edward Said Public Library in Beit Lahia, north Gaza. The news and pictures came through just three days after Gazans were allowed to return to north Gaza." The elimination of his libraries prompted Abu Toha to say, "The destruction of the Edward Said Public Library is just one war crime committed against Gaza and Gazans in the past 15 months. The obliteration of Gaza's universities, schools, cultural centers as well as religious sites must be condemned." Despite the horrible destruction unleashed upon his and countless other Gazan libraries, Abu Toha wants the libraries to rise again. He writes, "I'm committed to rebuilding the library, its two branches, and even expand the project to build one in Rafah and another in Khan Younis. My only two concerns now are whether I can get books into Gaza, and also whether I will find children who are convinced that this is safe and important to visit the library."

TWO BOOKSTORES

Even in the face of Israel's assault on Palestinian authors, books, and stories, Gaza does have people doing the heroic work of building community around new books. Indeed, it's hard to stop a bookseller. The Samir Mansour Bookstore was at the absolute center of Gaza's literary life. Like City Lights, The Samir Mansour Bookstore was a publisher and a bookseller, both publishing Gazans and providing them with whatever new books they could weasel through Israel's physical and intellectual blockades. Abu Toha, who would certainly know something like this, claims that "The Samir Mansour Bookstore played a significant role in promoting culture and resilience in Gaza," adding that "every single student—not to say every reader—in Gaza has stepped in and used the bookstore since it opened in 1999."[183] Like so many bookstores around the world, the Samir Mansour Bookstore not only sold books but made them. And they not only made books but they created community, providing a gathering space and social hub for the Gaza literary scene. You could say it was the City Lights of Gaza. In May 2021, the Samir Mansour Bookstore was completely destroyed by Israeli bombs. Images of the bookstore-turned-rubble spread around the world, inspiring a fundraising campaign to help Mansour rebuild. Rebuild he did: In 2022, the new Samir Mansour Bookshop opened, twice its original size. Despite Israeli restrictions, Mansour managed to stock the store with 400,000 books in a variety of languages.[184] A year later, less than a week into Israel's 2023 assault on Gaza, the bookstore was again left totally inoperable thanks to Israeli bombs. Not only was the bookstore a hub of Gazan literary life, it was perhaps the only Palestinian publisher in Palestine.

Even in the midst of the early-2025 ceasefire, Israel's attacks on Palestinian bookstores and libraries didn't cease, and they weren't even limited to Gaza. Another Palestinian literary icon was the Educational Bookshop, which occupied two neighboring storefronts in East Jerusalem. For more than 40 years, the Educational Bookshop has served as the nexus of several different readers and literary communities across the Middle East. One journalist claims that "the institution is now considered one of the leading booksellers in the Middle East, frequented by journalists, researchers, diplomats, and tourists for their extensive collection of books about the politics and history of Israel-Palestine in English, Arabic, and other languages."[185] It also hosted cultural events, becoming especially popular among researchers, journalists and foreign diplomats."[186] For decades, owner Mahmoud Muna and his team dedicatedly operated this hub of stories and readers through wartime and peacetime, distributing vital stories and gaining an international following.

On February 9, 2025, Israeli police raided both locations of the Educational Bookshop. The police ransacked the shelves, spilling books all over the place. They confiscated several titles. They detained store owner Mahmoud Muna and his nephew Ahmed and forced the store to close. They prohibited the Munas from returning to their store for 20 days. According to news reports, "Mahmoud's wife May Muna said the soldiers picked out books with Palestinian titles or flags, 'without knowing what any of them meant.' She said they used Google Translate on some the Arabic titles to see what they meant before carting them away in plastic bags." The whole operation was careless and dubious in its legality. In an interview after the arrest, Mahmoud Muna says, "The Israeli police came to the bookshop with a search warrant, which didn't give them the right to arrest us. So, at some point, they changed their accusations against us from 'incitement' to 'disturbing public order'—because under that charge, they can detain people."[187]

On top of being shifty about the search warrant, it appears that the cops didn't recognize that the books had already been investigated and cleared by Israeli censors when they were imported from abroad. It is unclear what made Israeli authorities reverse course on the legality of these books, but a lawyer for the Muna family expressed strong suspicion that the attack was political rather than legal.[188] On top of being legally shifty and politically motivated with their search, the Israeli police were also careless with the books. According to Mahmoud Muna, 250 books were gathered up by the police and shoved into plastic bags. He offered boxes so they could transport the books properly, but the police refused his offer. When all but eight of the books were returned, many were irreparably damaged due to the police's mishandling. Mahmoud Muna says, "What really hurt me was the lack of respect for the books. There are proper ways to handle, transport, and treat books. But throwing them into garbage bags like old clothes or shoes is neither professional nor respectful."[189] Take it from my time as a bookseller: Any bookseller is going to get mad about damaged books. But add to this the difficulty and expense of getting books into Palestine; these books quite literally were treasures. But that's not even the most devastating part of the raid; Mahmoud Muna's 11-year-old daughter was in the store to witness her father's arrest. He says, "Leila is still traumatized. She seems to be doing better since we returned [from jail], but I know these things can stay with people for a long time."[190]

Mere weeks later, 10 Israeli police officers again raided the bookshop, again using Google Translate as their only guide to which books should be confiscated, again arresting one of the owners. This time, as they took bookshop owner Imad Muna (Ahmad's father) to a police station for questioning, the police officers locked the store and confiscated the keys. Muna and the keys were eventually released, but the books were not.[191]

Israeli forces targeted at least two bookstores during the post-October 7 assault: East Jerusalem's Educational Bookshop and Gaza's Samir Mansour Bookshop in Gaza. Both were attacked multiple times. It's essential to understand that both bookshops were more than just book vendors, they were the centers of intellectual and literary community in Palestine. Israel wasn't just attacking bookshops; they were attacking Palestinians' rights to peacefully assemble and form literary community. The right for Palestinians to tell their own stories. In the case of the Educational Bookshop, it wasn't just Palestinians, either. Countless diplomats found a literary home at the chains' locations, as well. Many of those diplomats rallied in support of the Munas in the wake of their arrest. Not only did the Educational Bookshop provide a literary community for Palestinians, but they also facilitated a space to share Palestinian stories with the rest of the world. Perhaps it is for this exact reason that Israeli forces raided the shops.

One thing the case of the Educational Bookshop highlights is that book banners use the same strategies everywhere: all it takes to ban a book is a certain word in its title or a certain picture on its cover. A parent in Florida can look up the word "transgender" in a school library's database and challenge everything that appears. An Israeli cop can confiscate all the books with Palestinian flags on the cover and arrest the people selling them under trumped-up charges of disturbing the peace or abetting terrorist organizations. By the same malignant logic that declares any book that describes sex at all to be pornography, any Palestinian author is automatically a Hamas sympathizer. Additionally, American book banners and Israeli cops share another tactic: a façade of concern for children. One of the books that led to the incitement charges against the Munas was a children's coloring book.

ATEF ABU SAIF

An American small press cannot rebuild Gaza. But, in the wake of Israel's assault on Palestine's literary infrastructure, American publishers can ensure broad access to Gaza's authors—of course, City Lights is doing so with Mosab Abu Toha's poetry. Another example of an American press working to ensure that Gazan writers are heard is Boston's Beacon Press, who in March 2024 released *Don't Look Left: A Diary of a Genocide* by Atef Abu Saif. The book is remarkable: it is the first book to reach publication that was written in Gaza during Israel's post-October 7 assault. Abu Saif, born in the same Jabalia camp as Mosab Abu Toha's mother, lives in the West Bank and is the minister of culture for the Palestinian Authority. *Don't Look Left* is not the first time he's written a memoir during wartime; his first book, also published in the U.S. by Beacon Press, is *The Drone Eats with Me*, a diary of Israel's 2014 assault on Gaza (the same assault that destroyed the admin building at Abu Toha's university).

Both of Abu Saif's memoirs are harrowing and vivid in their detail, but 2024's *Don't Look Left* is all the more affecting because the war that prompted its writing is still ongoing. Even the author agrees that the 2024 book is more harrowing; he tells me, "I never felt that I was going to die in [the 2014] war. That book was more artistic, a publisher and an author talking. So I was just writing. But this war, I had this feeling that I might die [...] I wanted to try something so in case I died, people could find it." *Don't Look Left* is as close to a real-time document that a book can get. The fact that Abu Saif was able to write the book at all is something of a miracle. For one thing, the book is a harrowing chronicle of his friends who were killed in the assault, many of whom were authors or journalists like him. Gaza in late 2023 and early 2024 was the most dangerous place on Earth for journalists and writers, and of course, poets too. There was Mosab Abu Toha's arrest and beating. And, of course, there was the story of beloved poet Refaat Alareer and the daughter he wrote his famous poem for both being killed. According to Atef Abu Saif, Alareer "was deliberately targeted, 'surgically bombed out of the entire building.' His killing came after weeks of death threats that Refaat received online and by phone from Israeli accounts."[192] To just be a writer in Gaza in 2023 and 2024 could be lethal, so that makes it all the more remarkable that Atef Abu Saif was able to publish a full-fledged memoir a mere six months after the beginning of the onslaught.

In many ways, *Don't Look Left* is a book about the difficulty of writing a book under the genocidal conditions in Gaza. Much of the action of the daily diaristic chapters involves searching for food, shelter, and cell service. Some days involve trying to excavate bodies, dead or alive, from beneath rubble. Other days, he mourns the killing of Gaza's scholastic and literary life. He mourns the bombing of the Samir Mansour bookstore, writing that "now books and crockery lie scattered among the ruins . . . A year ago, I inaugurated the [bookstore's] new building with all its new stock. Now it lies in ruins, and the world stands silent."[193] He also mourns his personal library: "I wonder what has happened to all my books, I have built up a veritable library there over the last 35 years. Is it now buried under rubble? [. . .] Books that made me the writer, and the person I am today. Every one of them has a place in my heart and formed a part of my intellectual growth."[194] Elsewhere in the book, much energy is spent trying to keep track of family members and friends, but, as Abu Saif writes, "It's difficult to follow the news as there is just too much of it. All you can do is try to make sure you are safe, then look after the people around you."[195] This is yet another element of Israel's silencing of Palestinian writers and books: kill journalists, bomb the bookstores, destroy personal libraries, and finally create conditions that make it impossible for authors to write because they're too busy trying to survive. On top of all this, even if a Palestinian author can find a platform, the global audience's strong expectation is that they write about Israel's atrocities, which in itself is a form of silencing—Palestinian authors may feel limited in what they can write about. I'll admit this book is complicit in this pressure, and I hope my readers will ultimately engage with the full beautiful spectrum of Palestinian writing, not just the writing that depicts Palestine's oppression.

Atef Abu Saif is an example of a Palestinian writer who found a way to be heard. Even amidst the death and destruction and scholasticide of Israel's assault, he kept writing. Not out of vanity or creativity, but out of necessity. In one of the book's most stirring passages, Abu Saif writes:

> As I think about what kind of future this city faces, if any, I'm compelled to keep writing. Through writing, we can keep places alive, we can put down our memories of the streets that are now rubble, the homes that have now been flattened. We can not only stop them from being forgotten, we can create a map for how they should be rebuilt.[196]

And so *Don't Look Left* is a remarkable document of the persistence and clear-eyed vision of one Palestinian writer who refused to be silenced. Not only did Atef Abu Saif's writing persist in the midst of Israel's assault on Gaza's scholarly life, it was also published, and fast. It's a remarkable story, and a clear example of what people can do to protect books. The entirety of *Don't Look Left* was composed via WhatsApp messages Abu Saif sent to Comma Press's Ra Page, his friend and British editor. Abu Saif writes,

> My laptop doesn't work anymore. I've tried turning it on and off many times but to no avail. I suspect some water has crept into it overnight, as I stupidly left it out on a table in the gardens where we're sleeping. I've left it in the

sun to try and dry it out. This means I have to revert to writing these diaries by hand, in my terrible, barely legible handwriting. I wonder about how to preserve it, in case I die, and the solution I come up with is to read it paragraph by paragraph and send it to friends, and my publisher in England, so they have copies.

In Gaza in late 2024, sending these messages to friends abroad was no easy task. In fact, it was life-threatening. Abu Saif tells me that in order to send the messages that became *Don't Look Left*, "I had to walk to the Egyptian border to get Egyptian signal to send it, or to the Israeli border. And believe me, this was extremely dangerous. And many times shooting was around me. I had to run. I get the signal for half a minute, then I send it via WhatsApp to my publishers." Other times, to get a signal Abu Saif had to climb to the top of a six-story building, an obvious danger due to Israeli drones and war planes. He tells me, "Many times I feel like I might die this minute, but I have to do it. I go to the sixth floor of my sister's building and the plane is up there. But If I didn't do this, these words will not see the light."

Page and his Comma Press team quickly edited and compiled Abu Saif's dispatches into a publishable manuscript. It was a rare chance to publish a primary source about a genocide while the genocide was still occurring, but it would take speed and creativity to pull it off. Ultimately, Page saw *Don't Look Left* as a way to correct flawed western narratives about the situation in Gaza. He writes,

> The corporate media's coverage of this genocide has been guilty of biased framing at best and outright repetition of propagandist lies at worst throughout. If we allow our understanding of world events to be corrupted and spun by craven, compliant journalism, we can never hope to understand these events, even those happening in real-time, before our very eyes. Atef's diaries give us a rare exit ramp from this state of ignorance.[197]

Abu Saif agrees—he tells me, "Israel is launching different wars against the Palestinian people. One of them is the war of narrative. Israel wants the Americans to know their narrative, not our narrative." So that makes it all the more vital to get Abu Saif's diaries into as many hands as possible; as he tells me, "We want people to know about us. That's it. Not to hear about us, to know about us through what we say."

Part of their mission with publishing *Don't Look Left* so quickly was to raise money for people struggling in Gaza—all proceeds from the Comma Press edition are being donated to Medical Aid for Palestinians, the Middle East Children's Alliance, and Sheffield Palestine Solidarity Campaign (Khan Younis Emergency Relief). Not only that, but Comma Press worked with publishers around the world to publish the book simultaneously in 10 countries. The American publisher that stepped up to rush publication was Boston-based Beacon Press. The process of publishing the book in the U.S. started in December 2023, when Ra Page reached out to Beacon for help placing Abu Saif's diaries in U.S. publications. Then, in January 2024, Page and Abu Saif made the decision to publish the writings as a book around the globe and donate proceeds. Beacon was immediately interested—editorial director Amy Caldwell says, "I immediately said I'd love to be a part of it and would propose the book in house. My colleagues were uniformly enthusiastic."[198] Beacon decided the best way to get the book out in the world quickly was to publish it as an e-book: Caldwell explains, "The goal with this book was to get it out, to make the book available as soon as possible, and that meant e-book first. But we found that there was a strong demand from indie booksellers for a paperback edition."[199] Beacon publicist Perpetua Charles tells me that the initial enthusiasm about a paperback edition of the book came from a few bookstores in particular, namely Powell's in Portland, the Strand in New York City, Seattle's Elliot Bay and Third Place Books, Books & Books in Miami, and the Concord Bookshop in Massachusetts. But producing a paperback quickly provided a set of challenges. To go from nothing to paperback in six months is warp speed for publishing. For instance, I started writing this book in March 2024. I turned in the first draft during March 2025, and it came out in June 2026. Publishing *Don't Look Left* in paperback as a real-time corrective to media narrative required creativity. Everything that goes into a book—cover, editing, layout, publicity, release plans—happened much more quickly than usual to get *Don't Look Left* onto bookstore shelves.

Of course, to publish around the world simultaneously meant translating quickly, too. Tadeu Breda, publisher at Brazilian publisher Elefante Editions, nonetheless jumped on the opportunity (full disclosure: Elefante published the Portuguese edition of my book *How to Resist Amazon and Why*). In an email he tells me, "Ra Page, from Comma Press, wrote to me in January 2024 presenting the project and inviting Elefante to be the Portuguese language partner on the international effort to translate and publish *Don't Look Left* by Atef Abu Saif. I was on vacation but answered him immediately. I was desperately searching for a book like this." But the challenges—including a good translator available to quickly complete the work needed to put the book out in Portuguese—were nothing compared to the need to put out the book. Breda tells me,

> The genocide Israel is committing in Gaza with the support of USA, France, Germany, UK and other West powers (and the passiveness of the rest of the world) is the most important event of our times. It'll change the world—for worse [...] So, Atef's book is part of what we're calling an "editorial intifada" of Elefante, as we're releasing four books about Palestine simultaneously. With these books, we're sending a message about who we are, what we think, the political side we are on and what we stand for.

Such principled stands are a clear example of how publishers can contribute to the radical sharing of voices that are at risk of being silenced. *Don't Look Left* is a vital document, a real-time dispatch from a place where people are under attack, but so is their literary culture and life of the mind. Ultimately, according to Perpetua Charles, "It's a symbol of the resistance to have a physical copy of the book."

Despite the courage, resilience, and hard work it took to get *Don't Look Left* into the world, the pro-Israel movement has nonetheless tried in at least one public way to silence Atef Abu Saif's stories. In late March 2024, Comma Press announced plans to collaborate with Manchester venue HOME to present a staged reading of passages from *Don't Look Left* with actors like Maxine Peake and Kingsley Ben-Adir. Then, on March 27, the Jewish Representative Council of Greater Manchester (JRC) posted a letter on Twitter calling for the cancellation of the event, calling Abu Saif antisemitic and taking issue with the book's use of the word "genocide" in its subtitle.

Accusations of antisemitism are a common strategy for the silencing of Palestinian voices. Often, these accusations employ the International Holocaust Remembrance Alliance's (IHRA) definition of antisemitism. According to Shane Burley and Ben Lorber, authors of *Safety Through Solidarity: A Radical Guide to Fighting Antisemitism*, the IHRA's definition—which considers all criticism of the state of Israel to be antisemitic—"originally sought to create consensus among political, civic, and educational institutions to aid in combating antisemitism."[200] However, they write, the "highly dubious" language in the definition has "proven useful for those wishing to shut down criticism of Israel's unjust policies."[201] The weaponization of the IHRA definition—which the JRC was clearly drawing on to shut down Atef's event—has gone far enough that even the definition's authors are sounding alarms. According to Burley and Lorber, "Kenneth Stern, a primary author of the definition, has expressed his own misgivings, saying it was only intended to be a guide, not a legislative tool, and has been 'weaponized' by the political right."[202] To speak personally for a moment, I am a Jewish writer and I absolutely reject the weaponization of antisemitism to silence Palestinian voices. *Don't Look Left* is a vital act of witness, a clear-eyed documentation of horror and destruction. It is an important book. To dismiss it outright because it is critical of the Israeli government is to engage in blatant censorship and misdirection. Inaccurately calling something "antisemitic" is just like calling a kids' book about penguins "pornography;" it is a deliberate misuse of language that forces pro-book and pro-freedom people into making arguments that appear unseemly, even though they're not.

Further, in attempting to silence Abu Saif, the JRC used another one of the central tactics of book banners: to remove a single passage from its context and use that passage to attempt to silence the whole book. The JRC homed in on a part of a 2014 work where Abu Saif compared the IDF's atrocities to those of Hitler's forces. This lone passage, taken out of context, was spun into the accusation that Abu Saif was a Holocaust denier, and then used to try to silence Abu Saif and his book. Then, JRC employed yet another book-banner tactic in their efforts: appealing to vague, ill-defined "community standards" that only serve those with power. In a statement, JRC said that "giving a platform for Abu Saif's works would 'seriously damage community cohesion' in Manchester."[203] Such appeals to community standards are a hallmark of those trying to silence oppressed voices, from queer teens in Texas to Palestinians documenting the horrors their people face. Even those who claim good intentions—in this case, fighting antisemitism; in other cases, preventing children from accessing pornography—can employ book banning tactics to curtail the speech of marginalized and oppressed people. Criticism of the Israeli government is not antisemitism, and be wary of the free-speech intentions of anyone who claims the opposite.

Regardless of the history or accuracy of the antisemitism accusations against Abu Saif, HOME decided to cancel the event. But bowing to one outcry caused another. After the cancellation, Comma Press issued a statement that expanded Abu Saif's Holocaust meditations into their full context, revealing that Abu Saif had in fact written that "Hitler's crimes against humanity cannot be forgiven or tolerated. They may be unprecedented in history in terms of their ugliness," clearly the exact opposite of Holocaust denial.[204] The Comma Press statement went on to claim, "Neither Comma Press nor the author were approached or given any opportunity to defend themselves by [...] JRC," ultimately concluding, "This character assassination cannot be allowed to stand."[205] Many in Manchester and beyond agreed. More than three hundred artists signed on to an open letter demanding that the event be reinstated. Later, in early April 2024, around one hundred artists demanded that their art be removed from display at HOME, creating a memorable scene of a gallery full of artists removing their own work from white walls. The pressure campaign by artists worked, and HOME agreed to reinstate the event. In a statement, Comma Press declared the un-cancellation to be "a potential watershed moment in the campaign against the intimidation that arts venues face for showcasing Palestinian artists and voices," recognizing the larger free speech implications of cancelling such an event based on a misreading of a text and an appeal to undefined or status quo-serving community values.[206]

British curator Jessica El Mal was in the audience when *Voices of Resilience* finally happened, and she offers poignant recollections of what happened there. At least in her eyes, Abu Saif's direct and powerful writing was quite impactful when read aloud into a theater. El Mal writes, "At *Voices of Resilience*, however, the poignant performances showed us that when faced with such relentless grief, the true meaning of resilience is to retain the fullest capacity to feel hope and love."[207] Yet, despite the emotional power of the evening, shadows of the event's fraught history lingered: "The security measures on the night were arguably veering towards Islamophobic, and gave the impression of the audience and performers being criminalized. Despite this irony and disappointment, it is an important reminder of the threat that poetry poses to power."[208] HOME was completely shut down that evening, with all other parts of the building darkened. Barricades were everywhere, police were watching everything, and bags were searched. The whole spectacle—the near-militarized security response to the simple act of reading a plainspoken wartime diary aloud—is perhaps best summarized by an Edward Said quote mentioned early in the evening: "The power to narrate, to block other narratives from forming or emerging, is very important to culture and imperialism, and constitutes one of the main connections between them."[209] Abu Saif agrees about the power of words, and the subsequent impulse for those in authority to censor them. When I ask Abu Saif about the Manchester incident, he tells me, "This is how you censor. You create kind of inner censorship inside the reader, right? Don't read this because this will be as if you are participating in spreading antisemitism or Holocaust denial. This is a misinterpretation, but it's not interpretation." And so Israeli censorship attempts to target readers and writers, preventing the readers from accessing texts by mislabeling them as antisemitic—and also trying to prevent the books from being written in the first place. Abu Saif tells me that "through writing, we fight back not for our rights, but for our life." An attack on a people's stories is an attack on the people themselves, and that's true from Katy, Texas, to Palestine.

THE BUTTON BATTLE

Battles over who gets to say what about Palestine are nothing new. In 2002, the Toronto Women's Bookstore hosted a book launch event for the book *Women and the Politics of Military Confrontation: Palestinian and Israeli Gendered Narratives of Dislocation.* As part of their promotion for the event, the bookstore staff made pins decorated with a women's symbol superimposed onto the Palestinian flag. The buttons read, "Women Against the Occupation." A regular customer noticed the buttons and asked that they be removed. The bookstore staff refused. The customer then began to spread word and the situation snowballed. The store happened to be the official bookseller for an upcoming conference on queerness and Judaism, at least until the conference cancelled the contract amid the outcry about the pins. Other Jewish-oriented events with the bookstore were cancelled. The phone started ringing all day at the store with angry calls, many from people who weren't in the bookstore's community or familiar with what the store did. Eventually, amid a swarm of denouncements in newspapers and synagogues, the Canadian Jewish Congress requested that the store sell a second button, this one with an Israeli flag and the message "Stop Suicide Bombings." When the store refused to engage in such bothsidesism, the CJC upped their opposition into an outright boycott. The boycott lasted for months, and it's clear that the pain still lingers for Anjula Gogia, former manager of Toronto Women's Bookstore and current manager of Toronto's Another Story Bookshop.

Gogia is animated and earnest as she shares this story with me over Lebanese food down the street from Another Story in April 2024. She tells me, "I'm proud of the work that I've done, both with the Women's Bookstore and here at Another Story. I think back when the boycott happened at the Women's Bookstore, no other bookstore came to support us. We were out there on our own. No other local Toronto bookstore ever called me, even behind the scenes to say, *Hey, really sorry that this is happening.*" When October 7 happened, Gogia was instantly brough back to the painful time of the 2002 boycott. She tells me, "I actually got quite triggered by that time, I'm sure, because it was so intense and I felt like I was reliving [the boycott]." One of Gogia's memories of 2002 was working to release statement after statement—perfectly crafted, thoughtful explanations of the

Women's Bookstore's positions that were nonetheless attacked the instant they were released. For this and other reasons, Gogia did not race to put out a statement in the wake of October 7. Plus, according to Gogia, putting out statements isn't even the core of a bookstore's job in a time of political crisis and tragedy. She tells me, "The statement is doing exactly what we're doing by having the books, promoting them, and doing the events. That is the statement, right?"

The night before we spoke, Another Story Bookshop filled a theater with a sellout crowd to hear Palestinian poet Fady Joudah read from his new book [...]. For more than 30 minutes, Joudah powerfully recited poems of grief, pain, and love to a completely rapt crowd. Joudah concluded the evening by reading the entirety of "Dedication," a long litany of a poem that crescendos around the contested phrase, "from the river to the sea." Of course, this particular snippet of language is another small batch of words, just like "pornography," "CRT," "woke," and "grooming," being stripped of context and accused of saying something it's not. But in Joudah's hands, the phrase became a vehicle for both pain and a toughened kind of resolve. As steadfast as Joudah's performance was—he stood without moving in the center of the stage, conveying a strong sense of gravity—cracks in the surface let strong feelings show through. It was a forceful, emotional, and unforgettable reading. Knowing that Gogia sees this kind of event as part of a bookstore's work in a time of tragedy, I ask her what her aims were in organizing Joudah's reading. She tells me that such an event is "a statement against what's happening in Gaza. It's a statement of witnessing and cataloging through poetry [...] it's a way for people to continue fighting against what we know is true, that there is a genocide happening, and that we can't just pretend like it's not. And that's the role of a bookstore: bearing witness to this world."

Long before my trip to Toronto, when I was talking to City Lights's Elaine Katzenberger, she told me she was working on publishing another Gazan poet (the book ended up being Nasser Rabah's *Gaza: The Poem Said Its Piece*, Pocket Poets Number 64). She calls her publishing of poets from Gaza "a direct result of the time we live in now, an attempt to do something." Pushing back a little bit, I ask her what really a bookstore can do in the face of so many threats to free speech, whether that be the bombing of libraries or the actual murder of poets. Katzenberger tells me,

> it actually happens to be commercial space that is the place to hold the line. In order to censor a bookstore or a business or a publishing house, you actually have to go after the books themselves and get those legally declared dangerous or obscene. And that's harder than riling up the community and getting them to say, *our tax dollars are paying for this, and that's why we can ban these books from the libraries.* But you can't do that in commercial space. As an anti-capitalist [...] in my own personal politics, it's weird to be arguing for commercial space. But this is where we come in as a bookselling and publishing community. We actually can do this.

From *Howl* to Gaza, City Lights remains an example of what can be done to defend books and those who write them. In court or in the court of public opinion, defenders of books by marginalized authors have their work cut out for them. We must keep up the fight, because sometimes it means life and death.

👉 HOW TO DEFEND BOOKS

STAND IN SOLIDARITY WITH BANNED AUTHORS

Contrary to any misguided "book bans sell books" theories, it is dehumanizing to have your books attacked or banned. Regardless of who you are, but especially if you're an author or an artist, try to find ways to show solidarity with authors under attack. You can buy their books or post about them online. You can put pressure on their publishers to do everything they can to defend them. You can bring attention to their fate. If possible, let them know you see them and stand with them. The other artists at HOME walking in and literally removing their art in protest of the cancellation of Atef Abu Saif's event is an inspiring example of what can happen when other artists show solidarity with banned authors.

AMPLIFY VICTIMS' STORIES

I first found out about the arrest of East Jerusalem booksellers Mahmoud and Ahmad Mouna through an Instagram post by American author Eve Ewing. The day she posted about their fate, Ewing was on the cusp of releasing a major new book the next day. She took a break from book promotion to highlight the censorious actions of the Israeli police, and to highlight the important work of the Munas over decades of bookselling. Her heartfelt reflections on the Munas and the work of bookselling in general—coming at a time when she could easily be promoting her brilliant new book instead—stand as an inspiration for what people can do in sharing the stories of victims of the right's assault on stories. Read the books, share the stories, speak up for people who the powerful are trying to silence.

DO THE WORK

I was really struck by Anjula Gogia's refusal to issue any statements in the wake of October 7 and her insistence that her store's work was all the statement needed. This seems like a valuable lesson when so many people show support for banned books through social media posts, T-shirts, and cute bookstore displays. That stuff is all well and good, but as these authors are at times risking their lives to get their stories told during an assault on their right to do so, what else are you doing? Remember, the first banned book display was at City Lights while Lawrence Ferlinghetti was fighting for free speech in court. Don't just wear your T-shirt, wear it to testify at a library board meeting. Even better, run for library board yourself and wear the shirt while you ignore the ravings of narrow-minded book banners.

CHAPTER 5: BOOKS TO CHANGE AND SAVE LIVES: PRISONS

THE HIDDEN BOOK BAN CRISIS

Perhaps the most out-of-control book banning crisis in the United States is happening very quietly. It features no grandstanding at school board meetings, no librarians being harassed, and very little news coverage. Nonetheless, it has all the hallmarks of a fascist anti-book campaign: small numbers of people deciding what a population can read, Christian nationalist politics, silencing diverse viewpoints, and the real threat of soft censorship. Many folks don't realize it, but the most long running and severe book banning project in America happens behind prison walls.

The United States imprisons more people than all other countries.[210] This vast population is subject to poor conditions, being forced into low-paid labor, and financial exploitation by the companies that provide computer and phone services. For incarcerated people, one potential bright spot in the bleak environment of American prisons is access to good reading material. According to a study published in *Open Information Science*, "People who have been incarcerated have described the role of books in changing and saving their lives, providing a means to maintain themselves under terrible conditions, and providing a feeling of community both with others who are incarcerated and with the outside world."[211] While serving a 50-year sentence, Hugh Williams, Jr. wrote a preface to a book by the Appalachian Prison Book Project where he says, "Having access to books literally saved my life."[212] Running parallel to the idea that books can be a literal lifesaver for incarcerated people is the inescapable fact that, according to prison literacy advocate Michelle Dillon, "Jail and prison censorship is the predominant form of state censorship in the United States today."[213]

The act of trying to control what incarcerated people read—and the often-parallel act of promoting a single Christian nationalist viewpoint to all prisoners regardless of their background or belief—is far from new. Until the 1960s and 1970s, many jails and prisons only allowed their residents to read the Bible.[214] The impulse to ban all books except the Bible behind prison walls isn't even totally gone—one Arkansas jail attempted to remove every book except the Christian Bible *in 2021*.[215] The bias towards Christian reading material for incarcerated people is reinforced by none other than the U.S. Supreme Court. In 2006's *Beard v. Banks*, Ronald Banks challenged the constitutionality of the fact that, in his high-security Pennsylvania solitary confinement, only religious texts were made available to him and other inmates considered violent. In court, prison officials argued that newspapers and other secular texts were easily lit on fire or otherwise turned into weapons. Despite the fact that a Bible can also be lit on fire, the Supreme Court ruled 6-2 in favor of Pennsylvania's right to deny all but Christian reading material to violent inmates in solitary confinement. While based in legal precedent, the bias towards religious texts is also easy for prison staff to enact informally. Kwaneta Harris, locked up in solitary for years, explains that "if we have been discipline-free for 90 days, we qualify for one book a week, delivered from the library."[216] However, Harris explains, "Whether we request a specific book and author or a generic mystery, romance, or humor book, the librarian always sends a Christian-themed book." When Harris challenged the librarian on this, the librarian's response was, "I'm called to save your heathen soul." This is not to say that inmates shouldn't have access to religious texts; religion is often a balm in horrifying prison conditions, and Bibles remain some of the most requested books from prison book donation groups. But the choice to read a Bible should be a choice, not forced. From schools to libraries to Palestine to prisons: book bans are a major weapon in the religious right's mission to advance their values and eliminate all others. The problem is perhaps most egregious in prisons, though, where Christian nationalists have a (literally) captive audience. Incarcerated people have no other choice or alternatives for reading material besides what the mailroom and wardens allow them to read, a situation that's primed for abuse and corruption.

The prison book ban problem goes far beyond the forcing of certain religious values onto incarcerated people. As capricious, widespread, and pervasive as the school book ban movement is, the prison book ban system is even worse. This often-arbitrary system revolves around two types of book bans: content-neutral bans and content-based bans. Content-neutral bans "restrict the outlets which can provide publications, restricting book deliveries to 'approved vendors' rather than family or Books to Prisoners groups."[217] Of special interest to this author, several states have content-neutral bans that basically eliminate all book vendors except Amazon. We'll discuss that in detail later in this chapter. The second type of prison bans, content-based bans, "restrict the content of individual publications, often for sexual or violent content," but also, "content-based censorship often extends to books that deal with racism, injustice, civil rights, and LGBTQ experiences of incarceration."[218] Basically, a prison mailroom worker can censor a book because the book comes from an un-approved source or it contains un-approved content. Two different ways to skin the same cat. Whatever the method, though, both forms of censorship have the same effect: drastically limiting the information and entertainment available to incarcerated people.[219] All told, according to PEN America, prison book bans "represent the largest book ban policy in the United States."[220]

One problem plaguing both imprisoned readers and the people trying to send them books is the unpredictable and cruel way these dual ban systems are enforced. A common and justified complaint about prisons trying to control what books can get to prisoners is how little transparency there is around the whole process. For one thing, the decision to ban a book often falls onto one person. Many of the problems with getting books into prisons are outlined in *Books Through Bars: Stories from the Prison Books Movement*, an essential book edited by longtime prison book advocates Moira Marquis and Dave "Mac" Marquis. In the book, they explain, "Whoever is assigned to the mailroom will sort through the incoming mail and judge, based on extremely nebulous definitions, whether a material constitutes a 'threat to safety and security' for the facility."[221] Dylan Pyles of Kansas City-based prison books program Liberation Lit corroborates this disturbing fact. He tells me, "It's very arbitrary actually. It is just somebody's call. [...] what actually gets sent back is always up to the judgment of whoever's opening the package to go through. And so, one person could decide that they want to let it go through and another person could decide to send it back." These bans—based on a single person's vibes on a single day—can turn into de facto permanent bans.

This single-person influence shares a haunting echo with the lone parents challenging hundreds of books in a single swipe. This excessive individual power can even be codified into policy: "In some states such as North Dakota, the final authority on censorship is a single mailroom official, who adjudicates whether each incoming publication is admissible."[222] This single-person with-ultimate-authority book banning system is often downright cruel: One Texas prisoner writes that "sometimes it's the mail lady who flips through pages at the door to your cell and reverses the decision [to approve the book]."[223] Imagine eagerly awaiting a book to help you cope with the depraved boredom of imprisonment, then *seeing* that book arrive at the door to your cell, only to have it whisked away. Even worse, this often happens for downright silly reasons: The same formerly incarcerated person writes that a *Good Housekeeping* magazine she requested was rejected because an ad for Depends adult diapers was deemed "sexual." It's hard to see this as anything but spiteful. But then there's the ultimate cruelty: leaving both sender and recipient in the dark over whether a book has even been received. In many places, "The incarcerated person and sender may not even be aware that the material has been censored, as facilities are currently under no obligation to notify an inmate their books have been banned"[224] All of this leaves a very small number of people within the prison walls with a tremendous amount of power over what information prisoners have access to. If you think that sounds like it leads to prison workers forcing their own values onto captive prisoners, you're right: Ultimately, "Prison authorities manipulate this imprecision to justify bans on any material that they may find personally unacceptable."[225]

The arbitrariness of the prison book ban system is one of the major things that greases its wheels. Because prisoners' access to books puts so much power in the hands of so few, justifications for content-based bans can be illogical, nebulous, or downright cruel. Many leave wide room for interpretation, paving the way for the kind of individual, spontaneous decisions described above. Liberation Lit's Dylan Pyles tells me that they can't get Missouri or Kansas facilities to accept anything with pictures. Arizona prohibits "depictions or descriptions that incite, aid, or abet riots, work stoppages, means of resistance, or any other behaviors that may be detrimental to the safe, secure, and orderly operation of the institution"[226] It's pretty easy to see how any book at all can be said to fit that definition. Similarly all-encompassing and vague is Arkansas's prohibition of maps, among other things: Their content-based ban prohibits "maps or drawings depicting a geographical region that could reasonably be construed to assist methods of escape or eluding capture, or otherwise be a threat to security."[227] One prison in New York used the same justification—books of maps can help people escape—to ban a book containing maps of the moon.[228] Especially vague parts of prison book ban policies often go after material "that is likely to be disruptive" or "is inconsistent with rehabilitative goals."[229] Again, it's easy to imagine this policy in the hands of the prison librarian in Texas who ignored all requests in favor of Christian books. She could just argue that pushing Christianity on prisoners is part of the prison's "rehabilitative goals."

These vague, easily misused policies are all over the country. Pennsylvania bans writings that "create a danger within the context of the correctional facility." Kentucky's prisons are barred from receiving any book with "obscene language or drawings" or that "contains any information that, if communicated, would create a threat to the security of the institution." In Alaska, publications and other mail can be rejected if they contain "information that, if communicated, would create a risk of mental or physical harm to a person" or otherwise should be "banned for good reason following an individualized determination by the Department." That last part is saying the quiet part loud: Prison book ban policies are vague enough to allow a single person ultimate power in banning any book for nearly any reason. This leads to bloated and nonsensical book ban lists much like the 800-book list that Matt Krause circulated in Texas, ultimately inspiring HB 900. It's fitting that in Texas, "under the pretense of 'sexual explicitness,' women's health books and self-help books about sexual trauma were frequently banned. Innocuous books such as dog breed encyclopedias and coloring books showed up on banned books lists. Texas was notoriously restrictive—the Texas Civil Rights Project obtained the state's banned book list in 2011 and found that it contained 11,581 titles."[230] When Kansas's list—created with no methodology or policy basis—leaked in 2019 it had more than 7,000 titles.[231] The end result of all this sloppy policy is the same as it is in every other environment described in this book: The book ban system is exploited to erase marginalized identities. As one study found,

> The justifications for censorship offered by prison officials are, far too often, skewed through the lens of power and control and frequently manifest as censorship of materials pertaining to marginalized identities. Commonly censored categories of books include Black history and fiction; Indigenous and Latinx publications; LBGTQ fiction and self-help; and publications written by and about incarcerated people.[232]

In prisons as in anywhere else, those in power know that books are essential and often lifesaving for marginalized folks. And few are more marginalized and powerless than this country's massive population of incarcerated people. What makes it even worse for them is their isolation: If a student runs into a book ban at their school library, they can possibly find another source for that book. Not so for those in prison. Ultimately, prison staff know that reading is a way for prisoners to claim a bit of human dignity, and that goes against their dehumanizing system. As one set of experts put it, "The extensive, and often arbitrary, reasons utilized to justify censorship efforts on the part of carceral facilities reflect their investment in maintaining systems of social privilege and oppression that have shaped, and been shaped by, terrains of information access"[233]

Even initiatives claiming to give prisoners freedom over what information they receive end up restricting the very freedom they claim to provide. Some prisons are giving up on print books altogether, opting instead for digital tablets that in theory provide unfettered (or, I suppose, less-fettered) access to books and information. But the tablets are highly restricted, with draconian filters and a low-quality book selection drawn from public-domain content farms like Project Gutenberg. Because the books are in the public domain, in theory, they should be free. But, "in 2019 the West Virginia Division of Corrections and Rehabilitation partnered with Global Tel*Link and began charging $.03 to $.05 per minute to read books on digital tablets."[234] That doesn't sound like much money until you take into account what prisoners are paid for their labor. At three to five cents per minute, the cost of reading this book would be, for the average-speed reader, around $16. If you bought this book at cover price (thank you), that's pretty close, right? But remember, prison wages can be as low as $.14 an hour. Taking that into account, the cost to read this book on a prison tablet (on the slim chance the tablet even allows access to a book like this) could be equivalent to the total wages from three whole weeks of full-time work. Double that if the incarcerated reader is dyslexic or has other challenges with reading. But these cost and access concerns have done nothing to slow the spread of the exploitative prison tablet system. Dylan Pyles told me that in Missouri, prisoners must use the tablets to access their mail. Nearly all mail sent to a Missouri prison is forwarded to a Florida facility where it's scanned and sent digitally to the pay-to-play tablets. Not only does this deny incarcerated people the comfort of, say, hanging a card from their children on their wall. It also massively complicates the ability of organizations like Liberation Lit to get books to the inside. Pyles told me the whole thing amounts to "pretty much a total book ban in the Missouri Department of Corrections."

GETTING BOOKS TO THE INSIDE

Perhaps it comes as no surprise that incarcerated people can't do much to fight back against this arbitrary and entrenched book ban system. For one thing, prison-set requirements for mailing books are complex and confusing. According to Marquis and Marquis,

> Prior approval is needed in many states. This is where a letter is written by the PBP [Prison Books Program] to the imprisoned person that indicates what exact titles will be sent. The person inside has to get this approved—which can be impossible depending on the relationship between them and the guards or the warden. That approval letter then needs to be returned to the PBP, which can then send the books...some [facilities] allow up to five books to be mailed at once, some only two. Some demand the books are new. Federal facilities have recently started requiring packages to be wrapped in white paper, rather than brown. Most jails do not allow free books. PBPS send invoices indicating that the books have been paid for even though incarcerated people do not pay.[235]

It's easy to imagine that the invoice rule is specifically designed to hamstring PBPs, basically preventing them from receiving book donations (which would be fairly easy to source) and instead rely on monetary donations (much harder to come by, especially if they're outside the traditional nonprofit industrial complex). All of these bureaucratic hurdles combine to make imprisoned people hesitant to even ask for books. But despite the challenges thrown up by the American carceral system, there's an informal army of dedicated volunteers working tirelessly to get books to the inside.

In the 1960s and 1970s, a series of lawsuits by influential jail-house lawyer Martin Sostre attempted to eliminate restrictive policies like those that allowed prisoners to read only the Bible. As the possibility for more diverse reading for prisoners opened up, informal groups of volunteers started forming to field and fulfil prisoners' requests for books via the U.S. Postal Service. Eventually these groups coalesced into a phenomenon called the Prison Books Movement. Marquis and Marquis call it "a diffuse, autonomous, and nonhierarchical movement who gather books others discard, and mail them to folks inside prison walls who write to us, asking for books."[236] Though the Prison Books Movement says that "sending books through bars gives us hope and joy," its members nonetheless face staggering difficulties in their all-volunteer work. They regularly bear the brunt of navigating draconian, vague, or outright inscrutable prison book policies. One example of the madness: Books to Prisoners Seattle decided to collect and share all 50 states' banned book lists for state facilities. A simple-sounding effort but doomed from the start. After years of work, Books to Prisoners Seattle could only collect two dozen lists. It became clear that "the information to fill the gaps on the resource page was simply not publicly available."[237] It's not even that the records are being shielded or hiding behind expensive or complicated FOIA procedures; rather, as former Books to Prisoners Director Michelle Dillon writes,

> it turned out that the reason we had significant gaps in our resource page for banned book lists was that some states would not deign to collect that information altogether. Some states, such as Alaska, simply had not bothered to create a central list. A book might arrive at a prison in Alaska and be censored, and the next day another copy could arrive and make it through the mailroom without any issues.[238]

This unpredictability, featuring book banning decisions that are often based on a single person's mood on a single day, raises a common specter in the book-banning world, already much-discussed earlier in this book: soft censorship. After all, how can a PBP respond to such unpredictable or nonexistent policies than to try to find the middle of the road? An amicus brief filed on behalf of a lawsuit by the Human Rights Defense Center puts it plainly: "Books are also regularly added or removed from banned book lists, sometimes even daily, and prisons do not always share these lists with book clubs, who are left flying blind. Because they are usually small and often staffed entirely by volunteers, and because it is costly to send books that do not reach prisoners, book clubs inevitably self-censor."[239] The specter of self-censorship arises so much as a result of book ban movements that I think it's safe to assume it's an intended consequence. After all, in the censor's eyes, the most efficient form of censorship is censorship that causes itself. The censor can just sit back and watch people become their own book banners.

In the rare case that a PBP can discern and follow a prison's book policies, of course there's no guarantee that books will reach intended readers on the inside. Arbitrary enforcement of policy is the norm in prisons and jails and is solely dependent on who is in charge at any level on any given day." To deal with these obstacles, Dylan Pyles tells me, Liberation Lit frequently follows up every shipment with a phone call to the prison mailroom, in addition to fighting each and every censorship letter they receive. It's possible to get books in to at least some prisons, but the amount of volunteer labor required to overcome deliberately obtuse mailroom policies can be staggering.

These random and randomly enforced policies ultimately serve to dehumanize incarcerated people seeking the lifeline of good reading material. Of course, only so much patience can be expected from people literally locked into such dehumanizing conditions. Such policies were one of the many root causes of the Attica Prison Uprising of 1971. In her essential book *Blood in the Water*, Heather Ann Thompson writes, "Attica had no newspapers, very few books to share, and nothing at all to read in Spanish [....] If a prisoner wanted anything else to read, he had to have it sent to him from the outside. And even then he might not actually receive the publication since administrators confiscated a great many books and newspapers they considered in appropriate."[240] Even worse, prison policies disproportionately targeted inmates of color. Black newspapers and other materials requested by the prison's vast BIPOC population regularly filled book ban lists. Even worse, prison officials threw away any material in Spanish, regardless of what it was or said, further dehumanizing the large percentage of Puerto Rican inmates at Attica.[241] This and a host of other cruel policies and neglect turned Attica into a powder keg that ultimately led to a four-day takeover by inmates in September 1971. So important was access to reading material that one of the striking inmates' demands read, "We demand an end to [...] the denial of prisoners' rights to subscribe to political papers, books, or any other educational and current media chronicles that are forwarded through the United States Mail."[242] Of course, the Attica Uprising story does not have a happy ending: A violent takeover of the prison by state forces and correction officers led to 39 deaths, both inmates and their hostages. Throughout the leadup to the uprising, officials thought restricting access to political reading material would diffuse tensions; rather, the denial of good reading material only inflamed the conditions that led to tragedy.

In the aftermath of the Attica uprising, government and police forces stretched to see just how much they could get away with while avoiding any accountability for the massive blame state forces deserved in the carnage of the riot's resolution. As just one example, the same state troopers investigating the riot's deadly and violent resolution were the ones who carried out that violence. They had free reign to destroy any evidence that didn't match their narrative of the tragic events, and they ultimately closed ranks to deflect blame from themselves onto the prisoners. This resonates with Dylan Pyles' abolitionist philosophy, developed in part from his efforts to get books to incarcerated folks. "I have this theory," he tells me, "that prisons are like a testing ground for the inhumane things that the state will do to the rest of us when they have the opportunity [...] so I think that we're only as free as people who are incarcerated." First books, then the very humanity of incarcerated people. First incarcerated people, then the rest of us.

So, the question remains: what is there to do to fight restrictive, capricious, and dehumanizing prison book ban policies? Despite the random and cruel nature of the policies, they're still policies and the facilities are still state- or federally controlled. That means a legal challenge might be the way to go to get books to folks on the inside. That's exactly the course of action Luis Correa and Avid Bookshop decided to take.

THE BOOKSELLER VS. THE STATE

Now a manager at Pittsburgh's White Whale Books, Luis Correa spent the beginning of his bookselling career at Athens, Georgia's Avid Bookshop, which I profiled in *How to Protect Bookstores and Why*. A softspoken guy in his thirties, Correa is well-regarded among booksellers for his handselling acumen and political advocacy. Many in the field, myself included, view him as a leader in the realm of progressive, political bookselling. We met at a pizza shop in Pittsburgh to talk books, jails, and the perils of trying to send reading material behind razor wire.

When Correa was there, Avid, like any other bookstore, occasionally fielded requests to send books to incarcerated folks. Whenever such a request would come through, Correa says, "There was just this built-in understanding that we couldn't send books to jails. That wasn't a thing." Even worse, Correa tells me, there was a widespread understanding that Georgia jails and prisons would only accept books from Amazon. The whole thing bugged him, as it should, and he had a low-simmering desire to figure it out. But then, as Correa says, "Covid happened." Bookstores across the country had to enter a chaotic kind of triage just to stay afloat, and specialized projects—like getting to the bottom of this Georgia/jails/Amazon thing—ended up on the back burner.

Years after first noticing the unofficial (or maybe official) rule that Avid couldn't send books to jails, a customer came in requesting recommendations for books to send his friend on the inside. Correa, doing what he does best, carefully curated a stack and sold it to the customer. The customer tried to send the books to his friend. The books were returned. The customer returned to Avid and told Correa that the reason for the return was that the books need to come from a vendor or retailer, not a personal address, a common feature of prison mail policies. Confronted again with the difficulty of sending books to the inside, Correa began to research. He found that particular facility's book mail policy and followed it to the smallest detail, eventually shipping the same books from Avid's address. The books were returned, with the instruction that books needed to come from an authorized retailer. The question of how to become an authorized retailer dogged Correa for weeks as he became entangled in what he calls a "bureaucratic circus." Eventually he got a person from the facility's mailroom on the phone.

I'll pause here to add that this story is not unique to Correa or Avid. I personally have been tangled in the same mess, trying to get books to incarcerated people from my old bookstore, the Raven, and getting them returned. Many, many booksellers have been caught up in the same circus Correa was at Avid. The difference here is that Correa is much more persistent than most other folks.

Here's what the person from the mailroom told Correa: They couldn't accept books from bookstores with a physical location. Because the store had a physical location, people at the bookstore could sneak contraband into the books. They could even, according to the mailroom worker, dip them in drugs before the bookstore ships them off (because every bookstore has a huge vat of liquid LSD in the back room, I guess?). Because of this, the guard said, the jail could only accept books from Barnes & Noble or Amazon. Aside from the fact that Barnes & Noble also has physical locations, Correa had heard separately that even *they* were having trouble getting books into jails. And so, Amazon had a de facto monopoly on shipping books into prisons and jails. Correa had reached what he thought was the end of his story; he tells me, "I felt that was kind of a dead end."

But then another customer came in and tried to send books to an incarcerated friend. After giving the standard "we can't send books to prisons, only Amazon can" speech, this latest customer mentioned that Decatur's Charis Books & More, a long-surviving first-generation feminist bookstore, had successfully sent books to the inside. Correa immediately called the folks at Charis, which eventually resulted in Charis introducing Correa to none other than Moira Marquis, who was helping coordinate PEN America's prison book efforts. According to Correa, Marquis quickly told him, "What they told you is bullshit, don't believe anything they say." She added that, based on her legal analysis and her work with PEN, the restrictions the mailroom had told Avid were tantamount to a forced limitation of the store's free speech. Correa's dead end turned into a path forward.

What followed was more persistence: In Correa's words, Marquis "talked to a lawyer who talked to another lawyer, who talked to another lawyer who all work in these kinds of legal challenges against book bannings in jails and prisons. And that got us in touch with the First Amendment Clinic in Athens at the University of Georgia." The First Amendment Clinic helped Avid develop a case for a legal challenge. Essentially, the resulting case was that, as Correa explains, "We as a bookstore give recommendations. And that's our form of expression, what we build a whole business model off of. Publishers can send books to prisoners as a way of their freedom of expression. Bookstores should be allowed to do the same thing." A year later, The First Amendment

Clinic formally wrote the complaint and sent it to the jail. The jail asked for an extension on their required response. They eventually answered the allegations with what Luis calls "really weak arguments." As this book goes to print, Correa is awaiting further updates on the case.

The fact that Correa and Avid got as far as official legal action is something of a miracle. There's a reason why many other bookstores don't get this far. Many reasons, actually. For one thing, legal action is expensive and no small bookstore ever has enough money to swing it. By partnering with The First Amendment Clinic, Correa and Avid could get around this because the Clinic used grant money to make all their work for Avid pro bono. Second, small bookstores are rather notoriously staffed by seriously overworked people. The work of keeping a bookstore like Avid going, the simple day-to-day stuff, can be enough to overwhelm even the most diligent and determined booksellers. But Correa was able to find enough of a spark to keep his fight going over many years, and even to this day. The slow speed of this, perhaps purposefully slowed by actions like the prison asking for an extension on their response, can make people just give up. But not Correa. He tells me the reason his fight is still alive is that "I am kind of being a little bullheaded about it and considering myself a prison abolitionist. I feel like this is one way my work can help make the lives of incarcerated people a little more humane. So that's why I was a little more dogged about it and wanted to keep going." An arbitrary, byzantine, and frustrating system, official and otherwise, is in place to discourage incarcerated people from reading life-enriching (or even lifesaving) books. The system also works to prevent people from sending those very books to the facilities that imprison people. Wardens, guards, and mailroom workers have an interest in maintaining this system, and their unquestioned but arbitrary power over it. Even if the system seems impossible to demolish, the right kind of activist can get around it, force its practices into the daylight, and make the lives of incarcerated people more humane.

THE VIGILANTE LIBRARIAN

With a system so entrenched as the U.S.'s prison book ban system (not to mention the carceral system as a whole), it takes all kinds of fights to resist. A crucial way to resist prison book bans is through the informal yet powerful Prison Book Network, where people are always welcome to link up, organize, and help get good books to incarcerated people. Another way to resist is to hold the prisons and jails accountable for their bad policy through legal action—we must not capitulate to the kind of power-grab that allows a select few to decide what a powerless many gets to read or know about the outside world. Finally, the same thing needs done here as in any other case of book banning: Put books directly in the hands of people who need them. Before he became a public face of libraries' resistance to book bans, Brooklyn Public Library head librarian Nick Higgins spent a lot of time doing just that. Before ascending to his role at BPL, Higgins oversaw the prison and jail program at New York Public Library. One day early in his career, Higgins ended up sitting next to Jim Huffman at a meeting. Huffman, who directed the NYPL prison program at the time, started telling Higgins about the work. Huffman told Higgins that his team regularly went out to Rikers Island with book carts, and that Higgins should join them one day. He ended up doing just that. He discovered a program that was "woefully underfunded" but nonetheless "doing miraculous work, just absolutely stunning." As Huffman started to mentor Higgins, Higgins fell in love with prison librarianship. He tells me, "It was sort of getting into a place where access to information is difficult at best and sort of absolutely, totally restricted at worst, and finding a way to open up doors and try to find where people are to distribute information. That is living the mission of a public library right there." Huffman retired and Higgins got his job.

As he ramped up his coordinating work for NYPL at Rikers, Higgins began to think in military terms about the opposition to his work from the prison industrial complex. He says, "For me, it was just about carving out space. It was like a risk board. I just wanted to take as much territory as I possibly could throughout the island of Rikers Island." Part of doing this was making some compromised choices just to ensure access to actual incarcerated people. He tells me it took "trying to do the best you could to build relationships with corrections officers and officials and make even some sinister compromises with your own values, just to make sure that they could open up a door for you so you could come and talk to somebody and ask them what they wanted." But Higgins persisted and gradually claimed more and more territory. The librarian took what he calls "my best Peter Parker, being unassuming while trying to get every piece of territory we possibly could. You're literally pushing book carts around through the prisons" in the service of whatever incarcerated people they were allowed access to. The hands-on Peter Parker approach allows for a kind of resistance impossible when going through prison mailrooms. Higgins tells me a story of being able to flout a capricious on-the-spot book ban that so haunts prison book projects and other folks trying to get books to the inside. He tells me, "This happened a few times. They pull a chemistry book [off the cart] and say, 'You know what they're going to do? They're going to build a bomb' or some bullshit, and you'd be like, 'Fine, put it in the bag. We'll take it off the shelf.' And then you just throw the book back on." When you're on the ground with your Peter Parker disguise and your trusty book cart, a one-person on-the-spot book ban can turn into a one-person on-the-spot book rescue.

Despite the Peter Parker metaphor, it was crucial that Higgins found people to share in his work. He wasn't a superhero so much as an organizer. He worked hard to broaden his coalition of Rikers territory-takers, explaining, "Everyone needs to see this because if we can't tell the story of what's actually happening in places where we lock people up and deny them access to information, their families, we don't know what we're talking about. You need to experience this, and you need to talk with people and build relationships with people and understand the impact." His answer was to recruit library students and volunteers to help him push around his carts and claim territory. Together, they made a ragtag team of folks working to humanize people caught up in the most dehumanizing system America has dreamed up. Higgins tells me, "Coming into a housing area and asking them about the books that they want may have been the only time that week that somebody had asked them their opinion on anything. It's less about a library and giving people books. It's more about a demonstration about how society should be. We just need to talk with one another and treat people like they're human beings."

The variety of approaches to responding to prison book bans—legal, organizational, direct—is necessary to answer all book ban attempts, and all attempts by the religious right to impose their values on the everyone else regardless of whether everyone else is interested in having those values imposed on them. We need to make sure books get into the hands of the vulnerable students being robbed of the right to see themselves in what they read. We need to show up and be a voice of reason in the halls of power where book bans take root. We need to wage a public war on hearts and minds through media, advocacy, and protest. We need to make sure institutions have good policies to protect intellectual freedom. We need to fight bad policies through legal means like lawsuits and challenges. And we need to do whatever we can to prevent the scenario where a few powerful people get to decide what countless powerless people get to read. There is room for every pro-book person in this fight.

👉 HOW TO DEFEND BOOKS

JOIN A PRISON BOOKS PROGRAM

Remember that one of the most important responses to book bans is to make sure their victims still have access to books. As illustrated extensively in this chapter, getting books to incarcerated folks is no small task, and much of the staggering labor required falls to volunteers. Volunteering with a Prison Books Program is a direct way to fight some of the worst and stupidest book bans in this country. Look up if there's a PBP in your area; I'm sure they would love your help.

STAY RESOLUTE IN THE FACE OF RIGHT-WING OBFUSCATION STRATEGIES LIKE FLOOD THE ZONE AND ENDLESS DELAY

Much like the advice to not obey in advance, do not be fooled or derailed by the right's obfuscation strategies. It's likely that prisons' book requirements are complicated on purpose; they simply don't want their residents to have books, or even worse, they consider their residents not human enough to deserve them. The fact that they think a book can cause a riot or a jailbreak or other kind of action is, again, a backwards but strong endorsement of the power of books. So even if the requirements seem impossible, and even if they throw random obstacles at you, keep working to fight them. This is true of prisons and all other forms of right-wing attempts to limit access to books.

TALK TO AND UNDERSTAND BOOK BANS' VICTIMS

In prison and schools and libraries and warzones, the people who cannot access books or otherwise share their stories are being stifled of a possibly life-saving creative outlet. It's vital to learn about and understand their plight, if only to remember how high the stakes of the free speech crisis really are. Several programs work to set up incarcerated folks with pen pals. In the absence of any legacy media or publishers willing to share their stories, many Palestinians are turning to social media to tell their stories—pay attention and bear witness. And don't let school board squabbles turn into shouting matches between adults where kids are ignored; listen to the kids and amplify their voices.

CONCLUSION: IT'S BIGGER THAN BOOKS

*I*n a cavernous hall in the Columbus, Ohio, convention center, several hundred librarians gather for a conference panel called "Unbannable: How Libraries are Ensuring Access to Banned Books." In this room and throughout the 2024 installment of the Public Library Association's annual conference, the mood is defiant and perhaps occasionally raucous. Here at the panel in the gigantic room, applause lines are abundant. A fighting spirit pervades the air. Solidarity, too: When the moderator asks those who've experienced censorship or banning to raise their hands, a majority of hands shoot up into the air to gasps and shocked reactions. Judging not only by the hands in the room, but also the presence of dozens of similar panels on the conference program, book bans are on librarians' minds. Among the conference's offerings are:

- Media Training: When Your Library Is the Headline
- In the Driver's Seat: Proactively Protecting Your Library and Staff in Challenging Times
- How to Say the Hard Things: Lessons Learned in Years of Crisis
- Challenging Times: Unite Against Book Bans and ALA's Policy Corp

- Debunking Misinformation about Trans Identities and People
- Cornerstones in a Culture War: The Role of Urban Libraries in Defending Democracy
- Pivoting to Meet New Censorship Tactics
- In the Trenches: The Battle Against Censorship in Louisiana Libraries
- Make the Most of Banned Books Week and Intellectual Freedom Programming

During my time at the conference, I'd categorize librarians' sentiments as less fearful and more defiant. They are looking for ways to fight back. In fact, that's what this panel is about. To the extent that a panel of librarians can be filled with all-stars, these librarians are all-stars. Up on the stage, about a quarter mile from my seat, are Chicago Public Library Commissioner Chris Brown, Las Vegas-Clark County Library District Executive Director Kelvin Watson, and none other than Nick Higgins. It is Higgins who says the thing that sticks with me most from the panel. From the giant stage he says, "First and foremost, this is not just about books. In fact, more importantly, it's about people and who has a right to belong in the community. And the books are just a proxy."

When I visit Nick Higgins in his office at Brooklyn Public Library, I ask him to expand upon his remarks from the conference. He tells me,

> So, if I had had time at the PLA conference, I maybe would've shown some maps that you can overlay on top of each other. One where anti-trans healthcare legislation is being passed. One where voter restrictions are being passed. One where anti-CRT educational gag orders are being passed. And book bans and all that. They sort of map onto one another, to be on the nose about it. And it seems like this is a broader, sort of philosophical, well-connected agenda [...] And the goal is to enshrine rights for some people and erode rights for others. And the

people that they want to enshrine rights for are oftentimes white and heteronormative.

The war on books is about the right to read, yes. Books themselves are important and at times even lifesaving in numerous ways I probably don't even have to mention to you, reader of a book. The ferocity of the attack on books itself is evidence of the power of books. That's perhaps an unintended side effect of the right's assault on books. Thanks to high-speed internet, mobile phones, and the general internet-driven devaluation of creative content, today's children have more access to actual pornography than anyone in human history before them. But the emboldened and fascist-leaning Parents' Rights movement is instead targeting libraries, calling books about sexuality and diverse experiences pornography even though they clearly aren't. In doing so, they have accidentally highlighted the importance of books.

But the war on books is one battle in a greater war: the war of who gets to tell their story, and by extension, who gets to exist. In the *ABA Right to Read Handbook*, Philomena Polefrone writes, "The claim of rooting out 'pornography' is, often as not, a smokescreen for targeting LGBTQ+ inclusion."[243] In short, attacking queer books is quite often the same as attacking queer people. In the introduction to *Trouble in Censorville*, Nadine M. Kalin and Rebekah Modrak write, "There's a covert agenda to this Orwellian revisionism: the demolition of the civil rights and social acceptance that African Americans, Native Americans, and LGBTQ+ people have fought for, through decades of struggle."[244] Again, it's not just an attack on books, it's an attack on identities. And the intertwining of eliminating stories and the identities they represent isn't just represented in the American "Parents' Rights" movement; throughout the world, attempts to eliminate a people are often simultaneous with attempts to eliminate their stories. As Atef Abu Saif told me, "It was humans. It was not political, it was not military. I don't care about what kind of tank is coming in. It's not my business. I was thinking about what happens around me. So writing was exposing the situation. It was offering the truth as it is because one of the main aims of this war is to hide the truth." The other aim, of course, has seemed to be to eliminate as many people in Gaza as possible. To erase Palestinians, one must also erase their stories.

One thing that unites the people who the religious right targets is their existence outside the status quo, which is maintained by that same religious right. It could be government forces conspiring to silence Allen Ginsberg's radical countercultural poetic manifesto, a document that directly attacks the status quo and the powers that maintain it. Art like Ginsberg's challenges the conservative, racist status quo, so its maintainers act to silence it and by extension those who practice it. It could be trans or BIPOC students simply wishing to see their stories reflected in what they read. Since their very existence challenges the heteronormative white status quo, those who maintain and benefit from that status quo—Christian nationalists and other factions of the religious right—seek to eliminate those stories as a first step in eliminating the very identities that fall outside their vision of what's right. It could be Palestinians, who have endured not only a brutal violent assault from Israel's military forces, but also a scholasticide that has decimated Palestinian libraries, universities, bookstores, and writers. The existence of a thriving Palestinian population who can tell and share their own story challenges the story Israel tells to maintain its control over the land between the Mediterranean Sea and the Jordan River. In the far-right Israeli government's eyes, Palestinian voices—and lives—have no claim to land or existence. The modern state of Israel was founded under the slogan "a land without a people for a people without a land"—the existence of Palestinians runs counter to Israel's founding myth. Any story that challenges that story needs to be silenced for the dominant story to maintain its power. Or it could be an incarcerated person, thrown into the world's largest prison system to have their very personhood erased. If the people that benefit from that prison system acknowledge the humanity and curiosity and literacy of the system's victims, it challenges the system itself. The American prison system only makes sense if its victims are not seen as human. So the system's victims shall not have access to any stories at all to read, let alone to tell. A story helps create an identity; if a story threatens those in power, so does its teller. To eliminate a story is to begin to eliminate its teller. And so those in power, often representatives of the religious right, go on the warpath against stories as a first step towards eliminating identities.

The fight against books (and therefore identities) is large, well-organized, and well-resourced. Just look at Moms for Liberty, who claimed to be funded by T-shirt sales when in reality huge amounts of dark money from the right-wing funding system flooded their coffers. This monstrous right-wing dark money Death Star is pointed at whom? Librarians. Novelists. Queer children. Refugees. Prisoners. The whole thing is a blatant example of punching down. The overwhelmed and outgunned victims need backup. They need defense. We must not let these victims act alone in the face of such a monstrous attack not only on their books but on their very selves. But what is there to do for an opposition that has no access to billions of dollars in dark money?

It must be noted that I'm writing the first draft of this conclusion in the first few weeks of the second Trump administration. It seems like every 15 minutes, a new flurry of bad news descends amid the violent and ruthless flood-the-zone strategy Trump is aiming to do nothing short of dismantling the federal government from within. Earlier this week, Trump tried (and failed, for now) to freeze all federal funding, bar none. And then, of course, there was the Department of Education memo calling book bans, which I've just spent 60,000 words explaining, a "hoax." Trump has taken steps to eliminate the Institute of Museum and Library Science, he's fired the universally beloved Librarian of Congress and in her place installed one of his lackeys, and he's guided legislation that cut all funding for the Corporation for Public Broadcasting.

It's strange to look back on the transcript of my interview with Nick Higgins from August of 2024. Higgins was in the midst of planning an October 2024 mass rally to gather support behind the fight against book bans, with the tacit hope of mobilizing votes against Trump in the following month's election. Knowing how that election went makes it awkward to recall Higgins saying something like, "My friend from across the river at New York Public Library tells me the best way to defeat a book ban is through the ballot." It's so easy to look at something like that, from a time like that, and feel disheartened. In many ways, Trump's election and subsequent actions have brought the book ban crisis, once a local issue, to the federal government. Even more dishearteningly, on my bad days, Trump's flurry of actions makes the book ban crisis seem like a minor thing compared to the administration's violent aims. But, I remind myself, book bans are just the start of an attack on the very identities of people who fall outside Trump's fascist status quo. The whole thing is a monster with many tentacles, and the tentacle with the firmest grasp on me is book bans. The monster must be defeated limb by limb by as many people as possible. And it's still possible, no matter how dark the federal government nightmare gets, to mobilize against the attack on books.

By the time I'm writing this, I've moved on from my career in bookselling to transition into a professional advocate role with the Institute for Local Self-Reliance. One of the reasons I wanted to join ILSR was because of their steadfast belief in local power—changemaking at the local level often comes easier than changemaking at a national level, and the local change can often inspire larger efforts. Remember that Moms for Liberty started local, with a group of furious Christian nationalist Florida moms, who then built a national movement out of that fury. So, while a right-to-read fighter cannot be blamed for being disheartened by federal elections, I would remind that fighter that the whole thing started with school board elections, and it can be finished there too. During those heady and hopeful mid-2024 days, Higgins also told me this: "You make sure that you can run for office yourself if you'd like, go to a school board meeting, be civically engaged, go out there and stand shoulder to shoulder with a teen who might be speaking for the first time at a school board meeting to talk about how these book bans affect them. Don't let them go out there alone." This strikes me as quite wise, and certainly more attainable than convincing Trump's Department of Education that book bans are real. Remember, this isn't just a so-called red state problem. The attack on books is happening in all 50 states, so there's a strong likelihood that a queer or BIPOC teen near you is thinking about raising their voice for the first time to defend the books that give meaning to their outside-the-status-quo life. Will you be aware that this is happening? Will you be watching on your computer? Or will you be in the room? Will you speak in support of them? Will you be in one of the school board chairs, listening to and legitimizing their words and voting in a way to protect them? Will you be overwhelmed by the mighty roar the opposition makes, full of sound and fury, or will you try to muster a noise of your own? Will you make the noise alone or will you add your noise to a roar fighting for marginalized people and their stories? In that window-filled, cluttered office high above Prospect Park, Higgins told me,

> Sometimes you have these school board meetings where some people from outside the community are coming in and making a lot of noise, and in a very anti-democratic way, causing a lot of fear for other people so they don't speak up because they're afraid to. We need more people to stand up and say 'that's unacceptable' and to find their voice. And also if there's somebody out there who's speaking up and they seem to be all alone, have the courage to stand up and speak with them.

Sure, Moms for Liberty and their ilk have a head start. We have some catching up to do. But though they're far ahead, we have the plans to the Death Star in our possession. Organize. Start local. Speak with many voices in unison. Turn a local movement national. Don't shut up about what you believe. We can use their strategy for good. We can get banned books to the children who need them. We can listen to and amplify stories of people targeted for elimination by state violence. We can stand behind a courageous teen as they head to the City Hall microphone for the first time. We can simply refuse to let the enemy steal our stories and our identities. We can write and read and make a righteous noise. We can—we must—refuse to comply to their reign of terror without opposition. We can create a world with justice for all, and we can start with the stories.

APPENDIX: RESOURCES AND ALLIES

Listed below are several organizations that each play a part in fighting book bans in the United States. Some are seeking direct involvement from folks nationally, while others are much more regionally or state-focused. Find ways to help on each organization's website, though I will say this: To a T, all of these groups happily accept donations and social media follows.

AMERICAN CIVIL LIBERTIES UNION (ACLU)

Founded in 1920 with the goal of protecting anti-war speech and conscientious objectors, the ACLU has defended free speech for more than a century. The ACLU has played key roles in protecting *Ulysses* by James Joyce (1933), *Grapes of Wrath* by John Steinbeck (1939), *Tropic of Cancer* and *Tropic of Capricorn* by Henry Miller (1950), *Howl & Other Poems* by Allen Ginsberg (1957), *Slaughterhouse Five* by Kurt Vonnegut (1973), *As I Lay Dying* by William Faulkner (1986), and the Harry Potter series by J.K. Rowling (2000). In recent years, the ACLU has taken up the mantle of defending pro-Palestinian speech. In 2024, the ACLU sued Columbia University over their banning of the campus Jewish Voice for Peace and Students for Justice in Palestine chapters. Also in 2024, the ACLU published a letter encouraging the U.S. Education Secretary to reject the conflation of antizionism and antisemitism. Despite these moves, however, the ACLU board thoroughly rejected a staff petition calling on the organization to oppose Israel's assault on Gaza and divest from its investments in Israel. This shows the difficulty that even the most avowedly free-speech organizations have in showing full-throated support for the Palestinian people; we'll see this again elsewhere on this list.

ALA INTELLECTUAL FREEDOM OFFICE

Founded in 1967, the ALA Intellectual Freedom Office aims "to educate librarians and the general public about the nature and importance of intellectual freedom in libraries," according to its website. The office offers first response services to libraries under attack, as well as consultation and assistance in attaining legal aid. They also offer some funding for states to help in establishing local or statewide intellectual freedom helplines. Finally, the office provides publications and resources like *The Journal of Intellectual Freedom and Privacy* and the annual list of top-ten most challenged books, as well as public-facing initiatives like Banned Books Week and Unite Against Book Bans. Miraculously, they accomplish all this with a very small staff of six.

AMERICAN BOOKSELLERS ASSOCIATION

Since 1900, the American Booksellers Association (ABA) has fought to promote and protect independent bookstores in the United States. The defense of free speech has long been a focus of the ABA, manifest today in its American Booksellers for Free Expression (ABFE) initiative. Highlighted elsewhere in this book is ABFE's publication of *The ABA Right to Read Handbook* and the tireless advocacy efforts of Philomena Polefrone in tracking and fighting book bans. In recent years, a small controversy bubbled up as any mention of the First Amendment was removed from the ABA's Ends Policies, replaced with language stating instead that the ABA will offer "support of [booksellers'] right to freedom of expression." The change, inspired by the ABA's reluctance to advocate for issues like revenge porn or hate speech, led some booksellers to believe ABA was retreating from its support of the right to read. Any objective look at the ABA's recent vigorous efforts against book bans would dispel this notion immediately.

ANNIE'S FOUNDATION IOWA

In 2021, three people were elected to the Johnson, Iowa, school board who had signed the 1776 Pledge. Sponsored by the far-right 1776 Action organization, the 1776 Pledge is a codification of typical Christian nationalist talking points about education, including mandating religion in education and avoiding "divisive" topics. Outraged Johnson parents sprang into action, flooding public comment and otherwise advocating for objective and fair education untainted by Christian nationalist ethos. Later, a loose collective of parents formed around the shared goal of keeping books like *The Hate U Give* on library shelves. Emerging from these efforts was Annie's Foundation, a new 501(c)(3) nonprofit whose singular focus is resisting book bans in Iowa. Some of Annie's Foundation's methods for accomplishing this goal include banned book giveaways and toolkits for Iowa teachers and librarians facing book bans.

AUTHORS AGAINST BOOK BANS

A massive nationwide network of authors resisting the attack on books, AABB should be the first step for any author wondering how to help. Any author can sign up, regardless of whether their books have been banned or not. AABB came together in early 2024, founded by a group of frequently banned children's authors including Samira Ahmed, Andrea Davis Pinkney, Gayle Forman, Alan Gratz, Joanna Ho, David Levithan, Sarah MacLean, Ellen Oh, Christina Soontornvat, and Magie Tokuda-Hall. The organization meets regularly online, has several state chapters, and features working groups like Rapid Response, Author Training, Author Support, Social Media, and Recruitment. A stated goal of AABB is to act as a hub for the many disparate groups of people working to fight book bans; on their website they claim, "We are the author wing in the larger fight to protect the freedom to read. We aim to organize authors on the national and local levels to support the organizations already in place. We are working with a variety of national organizations, as well as grassroots groups fighting book bans." Full disclosure: This probably won't surprise you, but I am a member of Authors Against Book Bans.

Book Résumés Project

A direct answer to the flawed and dangerous Moms for Liberty project booklooks.com, the Book Résumés Project aims to advocate *for* books. While booklooks.com found and highlighted the most salacious out-of-context individual passages from commonly banned books, Book Résumés offers resources to help book defenders establish a book's literary merit. It's an exact mirror image. BookLooks had PDFs you could print that used potentially offensive sentences and single passages to argue that the book should be banned. The Book Résumés Project also has ready-to-print PDFs that use expert testimony and close reading to establish a book's literary merit as a whole. These Book Résumés also contain links to reviews, lists of awards, and summaries of previous challenges. If the legal definition of pornography stipulates that a book must have no literary merit, Book Résumés are a key resource in helping to establish literary merit and (hopefully) convince those in power that even controversial books belong on library shelves.

Comic Book Legal Defense Fund

Formed in 1986, during a previous generation's book ban crisis, the CBLDF supports people facing book bans by paying legal fees and offering other help. Their work focuses on comics artists, but it is not limited to comics; CBLDF were key players in efforts to fight public library internet filters, internet censorship in Utah, and a California law that sought to add violence to the definition of obscenity. Put simply, CBLDF is the self-described "first line of defense when authorities intimidate individuals or businesses about the comics they read, make, buy or sell." Crucially, the CBLDF has united major publishers under the banner of fighting book bans: Their work is financially supported by such giants as Abrams, Scholastic, Penguin Random House, Oni Press, IDW, Diamond Comics Distributors, and VIZ Media.

Drag Story Hour

The most crucial thing Drag Story Hour provides is, of course, joyful and inclusive programming meant to foster a love of reading in children. But recent attacks on DSH and the books they read have required the organization to branch out into offering security resources, as described at the beginning of Chapter 3. In addition to their security resources, they also offer support for people who want to support freedom, parents who want to be good allies, and folks aiming to resist book bans.

EveryLibrary

Founded in 2012, EveryLibrary is the first national political action committee for libraries. According to their website,

> EveryLibrary helps public, school, and college libraries win funding at the ballot box, ensuring stable funding and access to libraries for generations to come. We also support grassroots groups across the country defend and support their local library against book banning, illicit political interference, and threats of closure.

A chief method that EveryLibrary uses to accomplish these goals is Fight for the First, their web platform that allows signature collection, social media publicity, and organizing tools for communities resisting book bans or fighting to save their libraries. In addition to this invaluable free platform, EveryLibrary also tracks anti-library laws, drafts and shares model pro-library legislation, and offers pro bono support for citizens looking to launch pro-library ballot initiatives. They are building an impressive record of success: EveryLibrary has supported 135 ballot initiatives, and they count 106 of them as wins.

FLORIDA FREEDOM TO READ PROJECT

Formed in early 2022 in the shadow of Moms for Liberty's meteoric rise, the Florida Freedom to Read Project (FFTRP) aims to unite parent-led groups in opposition to the so-called "Parents' Rights" movement. Galvanized by four early book bans in Florida—*Gender Queer, All Boys Aren't Blue, Lawn Boy,* and *Born a Crime,* the parents of FFTRP got to work. In the past few years, according to their website, the FFTRP has made a point to "attend school board meetings, send emails, use social media to build relationships, and report out what's going on around Florida." Their website is a valuable resource for tracking anti-book activity in one of the most anti-book places in America, and their show-up advocacy is making a difference on the ground.

GOOD BOOKS YOUNG TROUBLEMAKERS

When bookseller Tanvi Rastogi was working as a children's and teens' librarian, she was giving a presentation to a classroom. When she presented a book with a gay main character, the class erupted in a chorus of "ewww." To her regret, Rastogi did not interrupt this classroom bigotry to speak up for inclusion and diversity. Her failure to act in that situation led her to imagine what she could've said and what would've happened if she learned how to interrupt bigotry at an earlier age. These experiences led her to found Good Books Young Troublemakers. Now a bookseller at Ames, Iowa's Dog-Eared Books, Rastogi runs Good Books Young Troublemakers as a nationwide book club that aims to help teens and young readers "build (and flex!) their allyship muscles." Much like Moms for Liberty (except with much better aims), Good Books Young Troublemakers runs on an independent local-chapter model, encouraging folks to form these inclusive and educational book clubs in their own communities.

Moms 4 Libros

When Lissette Fernandez and Vanessa Brito met and struck up a conversation about Florida's restrictive anti-book education, they instantly knew they had a lot in common. Soon after that first meeting, the Miami Dade County School Board made it known that an upcoming meeting would address school library book bans. Fernandez and Brito sprang into action, mobilizing people to speak up at the meeting in favor of school libraries and diverse books. This effort grew into Moms 4 Libros, "a group of Hispanic parents and educators unidos against misinformation, the politically-driven censorship of libros, and attacks on public education," according to their website. In the years since, Moms 4 Libros has continued to speak up in favor of libraries in Miami and beyond, as well as circulating lists of pro-book candidates for local elections and partnering with other Florida groups to strengthen pro-book coalitions.

NCAC

The National Coalition Against Censorship, or NCAC, was founded in 1974 in response to the U.S. Supreme Court's *Miller v. California*, which ruled that the First Amendment did not protect obscene speech. Their resources include a listing of censorship incidents called CENSORPEDIA, as well as resources for challenged authors to help them know their rights. According to their website, NCAC serves "students, teachers, librarians, parents and others opposing censorship in schools and libraries; artists, curators and museum directors resisting art censorship; writers and publishers; activists and protestors; dramatists, filmmakers, creators of all forms of art and cultural production," as well as the 50 coalition partners that make up NCAC. With the second Trump administration going after "enemies," NCAC's work will be vital to protect everyone's free speech. To get involved, sign up at ncac.org.

PEN America

PEN America was founded in 1922 in the immediate wake of the founding of PEN International. At founding, both organizations' focus was on fostering fellowship among authors across cultural divides in the wake of World War I. Since then, PEN America has taken a special interest in issues of intellectual freedom, with their stated mission today being to stand "at the intersection of literature and human rights to protect free expression in the United States and worldwide. We champion the freedom to write, recognizing the power of the word to transform the world. Our mission is to unite writers and their allies to celebrate creative expression and defend the liberties that make it possible." PEN America's reporting on the book ban crisis was instrumental in the writing of this book, and their work on the subject has been essential and admirable for a long time. That being said, many activists and writers took issue with what they perceived as PEN America's inadequate response to Israel's genocide in Palestine in the wake of the October 7, 2023, attacks by Hamas. Internal and external protests throughout 2023 and 2024 led to the cancelling of the PEN America Literary Awards ceremony after more than half of the nominees withdrew their candidacy in protest of PEN America's response to Israel's aggression in Palestine, including the organization's decision not to issue a statement calling for a ceasefire. One of the incidents that sparked this protest was when disabled Palestinian author Randa Jarrar was literally dragged out of a PEN America event featuring outspoken Zionist Mayim Bialik. The protests ended up causing a leadership shuffle, with PEN America CEO Suzanne Nossel stepping down in the wake of the protests. It's essential that groups like Writers Against the War on Gaza, who helped coordinate the protests at PEN America, hold legacy literary organizations accountable. PEN America is too important to be allowed to get away with silence as Palestinian authors and journalists are murdered by the hundreds.

Publishers for Palestine / Writers Against the War on Gaza

Since a major component of Israel's war in Gaza is an attempted scholasticide destroying Palestinian authors, journalists, archives, libraries, and bookstores, it is all the more important for the book industry to fight back and advocate for the right of Palestinians to tell their own stories. Publishers Against Palestine, which according to their website is "a global solidarity collective of more than five hundred publishers who stand for justice, freedom of expression, and the power of the written word in solidarity with the people of Palestine," came together in November 2023 to unite publishers in solidarity and "to [create] spaces for Palestinian voices and those who stand in solidarity against the war machine." Writers Against the War on Gaza had their first meeting in October 2023 with a dozen people; their signatories have since swelled into the thousands, forming "a coalition of media, cultural, and academic workers who are committed to the horizon of liberation for the Palestinian people, and who organize against Zionism and American empire from within the imperial core." They focus on four central efforts: communications, cultural boycott, labor, and popular education. Both are doing essential work in trying to hold accountable a book industry that is too often complicit in imperial violence. Full disclosure: Microcosm Publishing is a member of Publishers for Palestine (for which I am ever grateful), and I am a signatory on a Publishers for Palestine letter urging a cultural boycott against Israeli publishers who are complicit in Israel's violence in Gaza.

Red, Wine & Blue

Red, Wine & Blue is a fairly ingenious response to Moms for Liberty because it also employs one of M4L's most powerful resources: moms. According to their website, Red, Wine & Blue "is a national community of over half a million diverse suburban women working together to defeat extremism, one friend at a time. We train and connect women from across the country of all political backgrounds—including many who have never been political before—to get sh*t done and have fun along the way." By recruiting and organizing suburban women, RWB is working to ensure that Moms for Liberty isn't the sole voice representing suburban women in the book ban war. Much like Valerie from Houston's Blue Willow Books, RWB encourages organizing through one-on-one, woman-to-woman conversations. Their focuses include, of course, book bans, but they also work on issues like "parents' rights" for everyone, not just Christian extremists, plus abortion access, women's health, and the economic forces impacting suburban women.

SOUTHERN POVERTY LAW CENTER
Founded in the 1970s as a law firm dedicated to fighting racial discrimination, the Southern Poverty Law Center has since expanded its mission into fighting hate and extremist groups across the American South and beyond. Their tools and reporting for tracking hate groups' activity are vital resources in the fight against book bans and hate crimes in general. As one example, the SPLC helped lead the legal coordination of the successful lawsuit that partially overturned Florida's restrictive HB 1069.

TEXAS FREEDOM TO READ PROJECT
Founded in late 2023 by three Texas parents, the Texas Freedom to Read Project has set out "to defend, protect, and preserve the rights of every Texan, especially public-school students, to freely read and access information and ideas." They dispel the notion that librarians are pushing pornography or that age limits on educational resources shouldn't exist, and their platform aims to return control over classrooms and libraries to teachers and librarians, not meddling parents. They correctly see right through the label "Parents' Rights," claiming on their website that "no one

parent should have the ability or right to restrict or prohibit access of information or ideas, they may find disagreeable, from all students." They fight the wave of book bans in Texas by tracking book banning actions across the state. One vital way this manifests is detailed reporting on book bans and related bills moving through the Texas legislature. Some of that reporting was supremely helpful in writing this book.

Unite Against Book Bans

One of the most visible national organizations fighting book bans and censorship, Unite Against Book Bans is a coalition of 200-plus groups spearheaded by the American Library Association. The coalition includes publishers, charitable foundations, and entities like the ACLU, ABFE (American Booksellers for Free Expression), We Need Diverse Books, The National Education Association, and several groups from this appendix including the NCAC and PEN America. According to their website, UABB "strives to stop the removal of reading materials from America's libraries and schools, which has soared to record highs in recent years. Unite is working to defeat the vocal minority that seeks to impose their views on others by restricting the First Amendment right to read freely." Initiatives have included the first Freedom to Read Day of Action in October 2024, and the creation of the Book Resumes Project described above. They've also created an action toolkit "with voter-tested, nonpartisan talking points, tips for contacting decision makers and working with media, grassroots organizing ideas, and more," according to their website. Crucially, they also provide targeted messaging for communities in book ban crisis, as well as individualized advice for what those communities can do. Perhaps the largest and most prominent of the initiatives springing up in response to the book bans crisis, Unite Against Book Bans has the potential to make a serious splash based on the strength and breadth of their coalition.

ACKNOWLEDGEMENTS

My deepest thanks to the people who answered my questions during the writing of this book:

Perpetua Charles, Luis Correa, Anjula Gogia, Lauren Groff, Jonathan Hamilt, Nick Higgins, Elaine Katzenberger, Valerie Kohler, Tara Lypsynki, Philomena Polefrone, Dylan Pyles, Charley Rejsek, Atef Abu Saif, Cameron Samuels, Emma Straub, Lisa Swayze, and Paul Yamazaki. Special thanks to Tadeu Breda for not only answering my questions but for arranging my appearance at the 2024 Flip Literary Festival where I had the honor of meeting and talking to Atef Abu Saif (not to mention for publishing both of our books in Portuguese). Thank you and eternal admiration to the booksellers, activists, authors, and librarians on the front lines of the fight: Your strength inspires me, and it should inspire all the readers of this book. Special thanks to the booksellers at Loganberry Books for giving me an early platform to share parts of this book at your big anniversary celebration. And what would I do with a book like this if it weren't for Joe, Elly, Lex, and everyone else at Microcosm? Thank you for being such a great home for this now-completed trilogy. Thank you to all whose labor got this book into your hands, from printers to warehouse workers to delivery drivers to booksellers; may their work be dignified and rewarding. And, as always, thank you to Kara and Jack for being the world.

ENDNOTES

1 "U.S. Department of Education Ends Biden's Book Ban Hoax," U.S. Department of Education, January 24, 2025, ed.gov/about/news/press-release/us-department-of-education-ends-bidens-book-ban-hoax

2 Kasey Meehan, Sabrina Baêta, Madison Markham, and Tasslyn Magnusson, "Banned in the USA: Beyond the Shelves," PEN America, November 1, 2024.

3 Lyta Gold, *Dangerous Fictions: The Fear of Fantasy and the Invention of Reality*, New York: Soft Skull Press, 2024.

4 Lyta Gold, *Dangerous Fictions*

5 Lyta Gold, *Dangerous Fictions*

6 Edward Said, "Permission to Narrate," J*ournal of Palestine Studies* 13:3, 35.

7 Barry Miles, *Ginsberg: A Biography* (New York: HarperPerennial, 1989), 183.

8 Ronald K.L. Collins and David M. Skover, *The People v. Ferlinghetti: The Fight to Publish Allen Ginsberg's "Howl"* (Lanham: Rowman & Littlefield, 2019) 151.

9 Cherkovski, *Ferlinghetti*, 91.

10 Barry Silesky, *Ferlinghetti: The Artist in his Time* (New York: Warner Books, 1990), 62.

11 Silesky, *Ferlinghetti*, 62.

12 Collins and Skover, *The People v. Ferlinghetti*, 14.

13 Bill Morgan, *The Typewriter Is Holy: Complete, Uncensored History of the Beat Generation* (New York: Free Press, 2010), 86.

14 Collins and Skover, *The People v. Ferlinghetti*, 14.

15 Collins and Skover, *The People v. Ferlinghetti*, 22.

16 Collins and Skover, *The People v. Ferlinghetti*, 24.

17 Collins and Skover, *The People v. Ferlinghetti*, 24.

18 Cherkovski, *Ferlinghetti*, 92.

19 Collins and Skover, *The People v. Ferlinghetti*, 31.

20 Collins and Skover, *The People v. Ferlinghetti*, 29.

21 Collins and Skover, *The People v. Ferlinghetti*, 31.

22 Bill Morgan and Nancy J. Peters, ed., *Howl on Trial: The Battle for Free*

Expression (San Francisco: City Lights Books, 2006), 2.

23 Morgan and Peters, *Howl on Trial*, 2.

24 Morgan and Peters, *Howl on Trial*, 104.

25 Morgan and Peters, *Howl on Trial*, 104.

26 Collins and Skover, *The People v. Ferlinghetti*, 34.

27 Collins and Skover, *The People v. Ferlinghetti*, 35.

28 Morgan and Peters, *Howl on Trial*, 107.

29 Morgan and Peters, *Howl on Trial*, 2.

30 Cherkovski, *Ferlinghetti*, 95.

31 Collins and Skover, *The People v. Ferlinghetti*, 36.

32 Morgan and Peters, *Howl on Trial*, 111.

33 Collins and Skover, *The People v. Ferlinghetti*, 39.

34 Morgan and Peters, *Howl on Trial*, 113.

35 Collins and Skover, *The People v. Ferlinghetti*, 42.

36 Collins and Skover, *The People v. Ferlinghetti*, 42.

37 Collins and Skover, *The People v. Ferlinghetti*, 51.

38 Collins and Skover, *The People v. Ferlinghetti*, 51.

39 Collins and Skover, *The People v. Ferlinghetti*, 52.

40 Collins and Skover, *The People v. Ferlinghetti*, 53.

41 Collins and Skover, *The People v. Ferlinghetti*, 55.

42 Cherkovski, *Ferlinghetti*, 98.

43 Collins and Skover, *The People v. Ferlinghetti*, 71.

44 Collins and Skover, *The People v. Ferlinghetti*, 70.

45 Morgan, *The Typewriter Is Holy*, 128.

46 Collins and Skover, *The People v. Ferlinghetti*, 70.

47 Cherkovski, *Ferlinghetti*, 103.

48 Collins and Skover, *The People v. Ferlinghetti*, 63.

49 Collins and Skover, *The People v. Ferlinghetti*, 64.

50 Collins and Skover, *The People v. Ferlinghetti*, 42.

51 Collins and Skover, *The People v. Ferlinghetti*, 42.

52 Collins and Skover, *The People v. Ferlinghetti*, 47-48.

53 Morgan and Peters, *Howl on Trial*, 131.

54 Collins and Skover, *The People v. Ferlinghetti*, 62.

55 Collins and Skover, *The People v. Ferlinghetti*, 69.

56 Silesky, *Ferlinghetti*, 76.

57 Silesky, *Ferlinghetti*, 76.

58 Collins and Skover, *The People v. Ferlinghetti*, 73.

59 Morgan and Peters, *Howl on Trial*, 199.

60 Morgan and Peters, *Howl on Trial*, 199.

61 Collins and Skover, *The People v. Ferlinghetti*, xii.

62 Morgan and Peters, *Howl on Trial*, 6.

63 Collins and Skover, *The People v. Ferlinghetti*, 103-104.

64 Morgan, *The Typewriter Is Holy*, 105.

65 Collins and Skover, *The People v. Ferlinghetti*, 42.

66 Morgan and Peters, *Howl on Trial*, 63.

67 Morgan and Peters, *Howl on Trial*, 107.

68 Morgan and Peters, *Howl on Trial*, xii.

69 Morgan and Peters, *Howl on Trial*, xii.

70 Kasey Meehan, Sabrina Baêta, Madison Markham, and Tasslyn Magnusson, "Banned in the USA: Beyond the Shelves," PEN America, November 1, 2024.

71 Jillian Eugenios, "The next chapter in record U.S. book bans? 'Soft censorship,'" *NBC News*, 27 September 2024, nbcnews.com/nbc-out/out-news/soft-book-bans-censorship-lgbtq-race-rcna172855.

72 Kasey Meehan, Sabrina Baêta, Madison Markham, and Tasslyn Magnusson, "Banned in the USA: Narrating the Crisis," PEN America, April 16, 2024.

73 Nadine M. Kalin and Rebekah Modrak, *Trouble in Censorville: The Far Right's Assault on Public Education and the Teachers Who Are Fighting Back*, Ann Arbor, MI: Disobedience Press, 2024, 80.

74 "Banned in the USA: Narrating"

75 "Banned in the USA: Narrating"

76 "Banned in the USA: Narrating"

77 Alessandro Marazzi Sassoon, "Jennifer Jenkins beats Tina Descovich in big upset: politics or pandemic?," *Flirday Today*, 19 August 2020,

floridatoday.com/story/news/2020/08/19/mail-voting-covid-19-and-brevard-politics-why-did-jenkins-beat-descovich/3399851001/

78 "Jenkins beats Descovich"

79 Olivia Little, "How right-wing media launched Moms for Liberty," *Media Matters*, 28 July 2022, mediamatters.org/critical-race-theory/how-right-wing-media-launched-moms-liberty

80 Olivia Little, "Unmasking"

81 Southern Poverty Law Center

82 Jennifer Jenkins, "I'm a Florida school board member. This is how protesters come after me," *The Washington Post*, 20 October 2021, washingtonpost.com/outlook/2021/10/20/jennifer-jenkins-brevard-school-board-masks-threats/

83 Jenkins, "I'm a Florida school board member"

84 Jenkins, "I'm a Florida school board member"

85 'Book Bans Harm Kids," *Scientific American*, November 19, 2024, scientificamerican.com/article/book-bans-harm-kids/

86 "Book Bans Harm Kids"

87 Heather Rose Artushin LISW-CP, "Why Book Bans are Bad for Mental Health," *Psychology Today*, May 9, 2024, psychologytoday.com/us/blog/well-read/202405/why-book-bans-are-bad-for-mental-health#:~:text=Key%20points,individuals%2C%20librarians%2C%20and%20youth

88 Heather Rose Artushin, "Why Book Bans are Bad"

89 Heather Rose Artushin, "Why Book Bans are Bad"

90 Heather Rose Artushin, "Why Book Bans are Bad"

91 "About," BookLooks.org. booklooks.org/about

92 Kelly Jensen, "BookLooks, Framed As "Objective" Book Rating Resource, a Moms For Liberty Joint" 16 July, 2022, bookriot.com/moms-for-liberty-booklooks/

93 Kelly Jensen, "BookLooks."

94 "Banned in the USA"

95 Matt Clevenger, "THS removes transgender-themed library book after review," *Miami Valley Today*, August 23, 2023, miamivalleytoday.com/ths-removes-transgender-themed-library-book-after-review/

96 Kristen Taketa, "A North County school district quietly pulled books, shut down libraries after a parent complained. Its policy dictates otherwise," *San Diego Union-Tribune*, July 23, 2024, sandiegouniontribune.

com/2023/10/21/a-north-county-school-district-quietly-pulled-books-shut-down-libraries-after-a-parent-complained-its-policy-dictates-otherwise/

97 Kiara Alfonesca, "How Americans feel about book bans, restrictions: Survey" *ABC News*, August 21, 2024, abcnews.go.com/US/americans-feel-book-bans-restrictions-survey/story?id=112991794

98 Stephany Matat, "Do First Amendment rights apply in school libraries? A federal judge said no," *Tallahassee Democrat*, 10 October 2025, tallahassee.com/story/news/local/state/2025/10/10/judge-says-first-amendment-rights-dont-apply-in-school-libraries/86585856007/.

99 Will Carless, "Oklahoma schools gig for Libs of TikTok founder; Does it meet state's own rules?" *USA Today*, 26 January 2024, usatoday.com/story/news/investigations/2024/01/26/libs-of-tiktok-chaya-raichik-oklahoma-school-library/72361037007/

100 Will Carless, "Oklahoma schools gig"

101 Taylor Lorenz, "How Libs of TikTok became a powerful presence in Oklahoma schools," The Washington Post, February 24, 2024, washingtonpost.com/technology/2024/02/24/libs-tiktok-oklahoma-nonbinary-teen-death/

102 Moira Weigel, "Christopher Rufo's Troubling Path to Power," *The New Republic*, November 27, 2023, newrepublic.com/article/176809/christopher-rufos-troubling-path-power.

103 "Banned in the USA: Narrating"

104 Jeremy C. Young, Jonathan Friedman, and Kasey Meehan, "America's Censored Classrooms 2003," PEN America, November 9, 2023.

105 "America's Censored Classrooms"

106 Katharina Buchholz, "Anti-CRT Measures Adopted by 28 US States," *Statista*, April 19, 2023, statista.com/chart/29757/anti-critical-race-theory-measures/

107 "Banned in the USA"

108 Ian Hodgson, "Florida schools got hundreds of book complaints—mostly from 2 people," *Tampa Bay Times*, 24 August 2023, tampabay.com/news/education/2023/08/24/florida-school-book-complaints-library-challenges-ban-department-of-education-bruce-friedman-vicki-baggett-parental-rights-sold-patricia-mccormick/

109 Ian Hodgson, "Florida schools"

110 Ian Hodgson, "Florida schools"

111 Ian Hodgson, "Florida schools"

112 Ian Hodgson, "Florida schools"

113 Ian Hodgson, "Florida schools"

114 Corinne Hess, "Elkhorn Area School District considering changing book policy after parent challenges more than 400 titles," Wisconsin Public Radio, December 13, 2020, wpr.org/diversity-and-inclusion/ elkhorn-area-school-district-considering-changing-book-policy-after-parent-challenges-more-400#:~:text=and%20Inclusion%2C%20 Education,Elkhorn%20Area%20School%20District%20considering%20 changing%20book%20policy,challenges%20more%20than%20400%20 titles&text=In%20what%20the%20superintendent%20said,the%20 Elkhorn%20Area%20School%20District.

115 Hannah Natanson, "The Post reviewed 1,000 school book challenges. Here's what we found," *The Washington Post*, December 23, 2023, washingtonpost.com/education/2023/12/23/post-reviewed-1000-school-book-challenges-heres-what-we-found/

116 "Educator Insights on the Conversation around Banned Books," *FirstBook Research & Insights*.

117 "America's Censored Classrooms"

118 "Banned in the USA: Beyond the Shelves," PEN America, November 1, 2024, pen.org/report/beyond-the-shelves/#heading-6

119 "Banned in the USA: Beyond"

120 "Banned in the USA: Beyond"

121 "Banned in the USA: Beyond"

122 "Educator Insights"

123 "Banned in the USA: Beyond"

124 Amanda Jones, *That Librarian*. New York: Bloomsbury, 2024.

125 J. David Goodman, "Texas Revamps Houston Schools, Closing Libraries and Angering Parents," *New York Times*, August 13, 2023, nytimes.com/2023/08/13/us/texas-houston-schools-libraries-takeover. html

126 J. David Goodman, "Texas Revamps"

127 J. David Goodman, "Texas Revamps"

128 "America's Censored Classrooms"

129 Amanda Jones, *That Librarian*

130 Amanda Jones, *That Librarian*

131 Amanda Jones, *That Librarian*

132 Amanda Jones, *That Librarian*

133 Christina Caron, "Librarians Face a Crisis of Violence and Abuse," *New York Times*, October 31, 2024, nytimes.com/2024/10/31/well/mind/librarian-trauma-homeless-drugs-mental-illness.html#:~:text=In%20 2022%20a%20study%20of,or%20aggressive%20behavior%20from%20 patrons.

134 Amanda Oliver, *Overdue: Reckoning with the Public Library*, Chicago: Chicago Review Press, 2022.

135 Christina Caron, "Librarians face a crisis"

136 Elizabeth A. Harris and Alexandra Alter, "With Rising Book Bans, Librarians have Come Under Attack," *The New York Times*, June 22, 2023, nytimes.com/2022/07/06/books/book-ban-librarians.html

137 Elizabeth A. Harris and Alexandra Alter, "With Rising Book Bans"

138 Alisha Ebrahimji, "Texas school district 'postpones' a Black author's school visit because parents claim his books teach critical race theory," CNN, October 7, 2021, cnn.com/2021/10/07/us/katy-isd-book-critical-race-theory-trnd/index.html

139 Kennedy Ryan, "Fighting censorship in Katy: Cameron Samuels '26," Brandeis University, January 23, 2023, brandeis.edu/stories/2023/january/cameron-samuels.html

140 Jo Yurcaba, "How a Texas student packed school board meetings to challenge book bans," NBC News, June 1, 2022, nbcnews.com/nbc-out/nbc-out-proud/texas-student-packed-school-board-meetings-challenge-book-bans-rcna28793

141 "The 2025 Legislative Session," Texas Freedom to Read Project, assets.nationbuilder.com/txftrp/pages/1021/attachments/original/1738268273/Report_on_2025_Texas_Legislative_Session.pdf?1738268273

142 *The ABA Right to Read Handbook*, New York: American Booksellers Association, 2024, 58.

143 Christopher Hooks, "Loathsome Dud: Jared Patterson's School-Library Bill Would Ban Larry McMurtry's Novel," *Texas Monthly*, 22 March 2023, texasmonthly.com/news-politics/jared-patterson-lonesome-dove-book-bans/.

144 Simone Carter, "10 of the Most Absurd Titles on State Rep. Matt Krause's 'Banned Books' List" *Dallas Observer*, 8 June 2022, dallasobserver.com/news/matt-krause-banned-book-list-10-most-absurd-titles-library-texas-legislature-republicans-14167741.

145 Becky Fogel, "Austin's BookPeople sues Texas over new law

restricting school library books," Texas Public Radio, 26 July 2023, tpr. org/education/2023-07-26/austins-bookpeople-sues-texas-over-new-law-restricting-school-library-books

146 Becky Fogel, "Austin's BookPeople sues Texas"

147 "Fifth Circuit Court Strikes Down Texas Book Ban Law as Unconstitutional," The Author's Guild, 19 January 2024: authorsguild. org/news/fifth-circuit-court-strikes-down-texas-book-ban-law-reader-act/

148 Fifth Circuit Court Strikes Down

149 "Ongoing Battle for the READER act"

150 *ABA Handbook*, 15.

151 *ABA Handbook*, 105.

152 *ABA Handbook*, 88.

153 Amanda Geduld, "Florida now leads the country in book bans, new PEN report says. How did that happen?," *The Miami Herald*, 22 September 2023. miamiherald.com/news/local/education/article279568719.html

154 "New Report Finds Unprecedented Surge in School Book Bans," Pen America, 16 April 2024, pen.org/press-release/new-report-find-unprecedented-surge-in-school-books-bans/

155 Andrew Atterbury, "Florida's drive to scrutinize what kids read is costing tens of thousands of dollars," *Politico*, 7 August 2023, politico. com/news/2023/08/07/florida-books-schools-00110181

156 Alexandra Alter, "Book Bans Are Surging in Florida. So Lauren Groff Opened a Bookstore." *The New York Times*, 5 May 2024.

157 Alexandra Alter, "Book Bans"

158 Andrew Bauld, "Disinvited: Amid Censorship, Schools Abruptly Cancel Author Visits," *School Library Journal*, 30 August 2024. slj. com/story/newsfeatures/disivited-amid-censorship-schools-libraries-abruptly-cancel-author-visits?fbclid=IwY2xjawFGkCtle HRuA2FlbQIxMAABHe-EvSQwNKi8ecpT-w-usahAxLQBSlETcq-rRQLbw5U8r5SYp1PWWdKu4LA_aem_t0k8Y9sJJvrHV-UHYHgy0A

159 Jessica Gould, "Books on Black history, immigration found in trash by Staten Island school, sparking investigation," *Gothamist*, 11March 2024, gothamist.com/news/books-on-black-history-immigration-found-in-trash-by-staten-island-school-sparking-investigation

160 Mosab Abu Toha, *Things You May Find Hidden in my Ear* (San Francisco: City Lights, 2022), 101.

161 Abu Toha, *Hidden*, 104.

162 Abu Toha, *Hidden*, 104.

163 Abu Toha, *Hidden*, 114.

164 Mosab Abu Toha, "A Palestinian Poet's Perilous Journey Out of Gaza," *The New Yorker*, December 25, 2023.

165 Abu Toha, "Perilous Journey"

166 Abu Toha, "Perilous Journey"

167 "Journalist Casualties in the Israel-Gaza War." Committee to Protect Journalists, June 3, 2024. cpj.org/2024/06/journalist-casualties-in-the-israel-gaza-conflict/#:~:text=107%20journalists%20and%20media%20workers%20were%20confirmed%20killed%3A%20102%20Palestinian,2%20journalists%20were%20reported%20missing.

168 Abu Toha, "Perilous Journey"

169 Abu Toha, "Perilous Journey"

170 Abu Toha, "Perilous Journey"

171 Abu Toha, "Perilous Journey"

172 Mosab Abu Toha, "Exporting Oranges and Short Stories: Cultural Struggle in the Gaza Strip," in *Light in Gaza: Writings Born of Fire*, edited by Jehad Abusalim, Jennifer Bing, and Michael Merryman-Lotze (Chicago: Haymarket Books, 2022), 153.

173 Abu Toha, "Exporting Oranges," 154.

174 Abu Toha, "Exporting Oranges," 154.

175 Abu Toha, "Exporting Oranges," 157.

176 Abu Toha, "Exporting Oranges," 157.

177 Abu Toha, "Exporting Oranges," 158.

178 Abu Toha, "Exporting Oranges," 158.

179 Abu Toha, "Exporting Oranges," 158.

180 Abu Toha, "Exporting Oranges," 163-164.

181 Abu Toha, "Exporting Oranges," 165.

182 Abu Toha, "Exporting Oranges," 166.

183 Abu Toha, "Exporting Oranges," 166.

184 Sherouk Zakaria, "Gaza's iconic bookshop damaged again in Israeli strike," *Arab News*, 14 October 2023.

185 Oren Ziv, "The Day Israel Came for the Booksellers," +972 *Magazine*, February 11, 2025, 972mag.com/educational-bookshop-east-jerusalem-raid-arrests/?fbclid=PAZXh0bgNhZW0CMTEAAaYxGIGml68T4x

cq3yxWqQGrGhD8vAmXc9LumRgeSZf2kOlukIWWJ-PSg9w_aem_
k21dh-XY38ALUz5P3dvX0Q

186 Mahmoud Illean and Natalie Melzer, "Israeli police raid Palestinian bookshop in east Jerusalem, claiming incitement to violence," *Associated Press*, February 10, 2025, apnews.com/article/israel-palestinians-police-jerusalem-bookstore-raid-rights-af721d98f55ec3103c2f90cf6013263f.

187 Elias Feroz, "'Selling books is not a crime': Owners of Jerusalem's Educational Bookshop speak out after Israeli police raid and arrest," *The New Arab*, February 24, 2025, newarab.com/features/jerusalems-educational-bookshop-owners-speak-out-after-arrest

188 Natan Odenheimer and Lara Jakes, "Israeli Police Raid Palestinian Bookshops in East Jerusalem," *The New York Times*, February 10, 2025, nytimes.com/2025/02/10/world/middleeast/israel-east-jerusalem-bookstore.html

189 Elias Feroz, "Selling books"

190 Elias Feroz, "Selling books"

191 Emma Graham-Harrison and Quique Kierszenbaum, "Israeli police raid Palestinian bookshop in East Jerusalem twice in a month," *The Guardian*, March 11, 2025. theguardian.com/world/2025/mar/11/israeli-police-raid-palestinian-bookshop-east-jerusalem-twice-in-a-month

192 Atef Abu Saif, *Don't Look Left: Diary of a Genocide* (Boston: Beacon Press, 2024) v.

193 Abu Saif, *Don't Look Left*, 37.

194 Abu Saif, *Don't Look Left*, 125.

195 Abu Saif, *Don't Look Left*, 105.

196 Abu Saif, *Don't Look Left*, 47-48.

197 "Six Publishers on Why They're Bringing out Don't Look Left," *Arablit*, June 21, 2024, arablit.org/six-publishers-on-why-theyre-publishing-dont-look-left/.

198 "How Beacon Press Worked Quickly to Publish Atef Abu Saif's Gaza Diaries," Beacon Press, June 21, 2024, beaconbroadside.com/broadside/2024/04/beacon-press-atef-abu-saif-gaza-diaries.html

199 "How Beacon Press Worked Quickly"

200 Shane Burley and Ben Lorber, *Safety through Solidarity: A Radical Guide to Fighting Antisemitism*, New York: Melville House, 2024, 42.

201 *Safety through Solidarity*, 42.

202 *Safety through Solidarity*, 43.

203 "Row as Home Manchester cancels Palestinian arts event," *BBC News*, 29 March 2024, bbc.com/news/uk-england-manchester-68693086

204 "Comma Press Statement in Relation to the Cancellation of Home's 'Voices of Resilience' event and Baseless Allegations," *Comma Press*, 28 March 2024, commapress.co.uk/blog/comma-press-statement-in-relation-to-cancellation-of-home-event-and-baseless-allegations

205 "Comma Press Statement"

206 Robyn Vinter, "Manchester theatre restores cancelled Palestinian event after protest," *The Guardian*, 4 April 2024.

207 Jessica El Mal, Voices of Resistance, *Corridor8*, 18 June 2024, corridor8.co.uk/article/voices-of-resilience/

208 Jessica El Mal, "Voices"

209 Jessica El Mal, "Voices"

210 Moira Marquis and Dave "Mac" Marquis, ed. *Books Through Bars: Stories from the Prison Books Movement*. Athens, GA: University of Georgia Press, 2023, 3.

211 Jeanie Austin, Charenko, Melissa, Dillon, Michelle and Lincoln, Jodi. "Systemic Oppression and the Contested Ground of Information Access for Incarcerated People," *Open Information Science* 4, no. 1 (2020): 169-185. doi.org/10.1515/opis-2020-0013

212 Connie Banta, Kristin Devault-Julefs, Destinee Harper, Katy Ryan, and Ellen Skirvin, eds. *This Book is Free and Yours to Keep: Notes from the Appalachian Prison Book Project*. Morgantown: West Virginia University Press, 2024, xii.

213 Moira Marquis, *Books Through Bars*, 43.

214 Moira Marquis, "The Legacy of Martin Sostre," PEN America, April 19, 2023. pen.org/martin-sostre-legacy/

215 Moira Marquis, *Books Through Bars*, 43.

216 Moira Marquis, *Books Through Bars*, 203

217 Jeanie Austin, "Systemic Oppression," 171

218 Jeanie Austin, "Systemic Oppression," 171

219 Jeanie Austin, "Systemic Oppression," 171

220 "Literature Locked Up: How Prison Book Restriction Policies Constitute the Nation's Largest Book Ban," PEN America, September 2019, 1.

221 Moira Marquis, *Books Through Bars*, 44.

222 Jeanie Austin, "Systemic Oppression," 175

223 Moira Marquis, *Books Through Bars*, 207

224 Moira Marquis, *Books Through Bars*, 44

225 Jeanie Austin, "Systemic Oppression," 172

226 Jeanie Austin, "Systemic Oppression," 171

227 Jeanie Austin, "Systemic Oppression," 171

228 *This Book is Free and Yours to Keep*, 60.

229 Jeanie Austin, "Systemic Oppression," 171

230 Moira Marquis, *Books through Bars*, 44.

231 Nomin Ujiyediin, "7,000 Books and Magazines Are Banned in Kansas Prisons. Here Are Some of Them." KCUR, June 17, 2019, kcur.org/government/2019-06-17/7-000-books-and-magazines-are-banned-in-kansas-prisons-here-are-some-of-them.

232 Jeanie Austin, "Systemic Oppression," 172

233 Jeanie Austin, "Systemic Oppresion," 174

234 Moira Marquis, *Books through Bars*, 43

235 Moira Marquis, *Books through Bars*, 5

236 Moira Marquis, *Books through Bars*, 1

237 Moira Marquis, *Books through Bars*, 47

238 Moira Marquis, *Books through Bars*, 48

239 Moira Marquis, *Books through Bars*, 46

240 Heather Ann Thompson, *Blood in the Water: The Attica Prison Uprising of 1971 and its Legacy*, New York: Pantheon, 2016, 9.

241 Heather Ann Thompson, *Blood in the Water*, 13.

242 "Attica Prison Liberation Faction, Manifesto of Demands 1971." Libcom.org, January 6, 2012. libcom.org/article/attica-prison-liberation-faction-manifesto-demands-1971

243 *ABA Handbook*, 64

244 Nadine M. Kalin and Rebekah Modrak, *Trouble in Censorville*, 18

ABOUT THE AUTHOR

Danny Caine is the author most recently of Jewish American Dream, winner of the inaugural Sarabande Chapbook Prize. He's also written four poetry collections as well as the books *How to Protect Bookstores and Why* and *How to Resist Amazon and Why*. He's a former owner of the Raven Book Store, winner of Publishers Weekly's 2022 Bookstore of the Year award. His poetry has appeared in *The Slowdown, LitHub, DIAGRAM, HAD*, and *Barrelhouse*. He lives in Ohio.

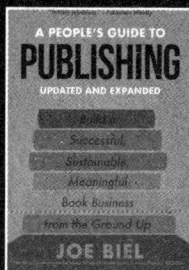